Unless otherwise indicated, all Scripture quotations are taken from the *King James Version* of the Bible.

Spiritual Maturity
Six Levels of Spiritual Growth

ISBN 13:9781481246873
ISBN 10:1481246879

Copyright © 2012 by Christine Carmichiel

All rights reserved. Reproduction in whole or in part without written permission from the publisher is prohibited.
Printed in the United States of America.

Christine Carmichiel

Table of Contents

1. Introduction — 5
2. Spiritual Maturity — 7
3. The Ministry of the Holy Spirit — 11
4. Perfecting the New Nature — 26
5. Seven Spiritual Keys — 41
6. Illustration — 44
7. Six Levels of Spiritual Maturity — 45
8. Level One – Born Again With a New Nature — 51
9. Level Two – Authority Over Devils — 56
10. Level Three – No Turning Back — 59
11. Level Four – Disciples — 71
12. Level Five – Sons of God Dressed for Battle — 75
13. Level Six – Agape Love — 83
14. Conclusion — 88
15. Appendices — 95

Are You Still Breathing?

Oh my friend, are you still breathing? Then you still have a chance to walk this out and fulfill everything He has called you to do.

Feed Your Spirit

Your spirit is not like your body. If you quit feeding your body, it will die. But if you quit feeding your spirit, it will continue to exist; it does not need sustenance to survive. It is eternal and self-existing.

However, if you do not feed your spirit, it will not quit existing – it will quit developing. (*maturing*)

You can remain in the same place spiritually your whole lifetime as you were when you were first saved if you do not feed your spirit.

(Prophecies reprinted with permission from Family Prayer Center, Dave Roberson Ministries.)

Introduction

In the spiritual realm, maturity is not measured by our age or works. It is measured by obedience to God.

We wait on God until He speaks, then we obey what He says and we begin to grow. When we disobey God, we stop growing. Some people have quit growing and quit pursuing God. Some have gotten offended. Some people thought they heard from God in prayer but later found out that they were mistaken. Perhaps you were taught wrong doctrine from those in whom you trusted. For different reasons, God's children have stopped growing. God is calling us out of the world now and into obedience again. There was a time when I also had strayed from His will. But it is never too late to get up and get back on track again. There is much grace available for us to finish our course. If there is a need for forgiveness, let us do so because we have been forgiven so much by Jesus. We must not waste these opportunities. They may be our last.

I am writing this book as a guide and overview of the Christian life. When times get tough or dry, we can look at the big picture, or look behind us and see how far we have grown or look ahead to see the hope that gives us strength to go on.

You are on God's heart today. He loves you passionately, and whatever happened in the past, He wants to reconnect with you now. Jesus is speaking to the Body of Christ also. Many churches have become religious and programmed God out of the services, taught doctrines of men and allowed our focus to slide away from Jesus and His presence. We are responsible to God for our own lives in Christ. We are the Church and we have not kept a watch on our spirit as we should have. Somehow the devil has robbed us of our intimacy with God. Love connects us to God and to each other no matter where we live or what the circumstances are. Jesus has given us His life, power and grace. He wants us all back in fellowship with Him.

As you look over your own spiritual growth as you read these pages, make adjustments, obey and be encouraged because you are growing more and more again. I believe there will be some answers for you in this book. It could open up whole new areas in your life you never saw before. It is good to step back and prayerfully consider your level of maturity. If you have lost Jesus along the way, then my hope is that you will see yourself in these pages, reconnect and be encouraged to continue again in passionate pursuit of your God. You will not regret it.

We need two things to grow: The Word of God and the ministry of the Holy Spirit. There are believers who have not yet entered into the power of the Holy Spirit or the heavenly gift of speaking in tongues for building up their spirit and they do not hear God as they should. Many believers are still being led by their soul (mind, will and emotions) and not by their spirit. We must know the voice of God and discern who is speaking to us: our own soul, the enemy or God. God wants to communicate with us. God is a spirit and He communicates with us Spirit to spirit.

If growth comes by obedience to His Word, then we must know what He is saying to us. He wants us to know. That's why He says, *"He who has ears to hear, hear,"* over and over again in the New Testament. Hearing God's voice is vital to our spiritual maturity. We hear Him in our spirit.

Spiritual Maturity

The Family of God

Christianity is a family, not a religion. We must be "born" into this family. (John 3:3) The love of God the Father is what connects us with each other. Our Heavenly Father is good, but religion and the world have painted another picture about our loving Father, sometimes even blaming Him for things that have hurt us. This is the work of the devil, aka the accuser, aka the antichrist. (Mt. 4:5, Rev. 12:10, 1 John 2:18) However, these false beliefs can be corrected on the inside of us. The Holy Spirit was sent to help us get free from these lies and past our own weaknesses. He will do this marvelous work of restoration inside our heart as we allow Him.

I noticed that maturity in the Bible is equated with the words "made perfect" or "perfected." Now, if you are like me, you can say that I am not yet perfect. But God wants us to be perfect. It seems that our Father has high aspirations for us. Indeed He does. He wants us to be like Jesus. So I can say that God wants us ALL to be perfect and mature. That is His goal for us. There is no one perfect here, but we are all going to be. We are God's workmanship. We began in a pitiful state, but we are progressing to perfection, step by step. And our Father is very patient to give us all we need to grow. But He has no pleasure when we draw back in unbelief or yield to our fleshly nature. Jesus overcame and we have His nature in us now. We can and must be perfected into sonship. It is our destiny and our inheritance.

Step by Step and Line upon Line

The ministry of the Holy Spirit is the only way real change can be accomplished in us. Most people who try to change themselves fail miserably. We need the power of God to change us. God wants us all to be like His Son Jesus. He has provided a way to accomplish this as it says in 2 Corinthians 3:18:

But we all, with open face beholding as in a glass the glory of the Lord, are changed into the same image from glory to glory, even as by the Spirit of the Lord.

Glory to glory means step by step in levels as we can tolerate the change from a soul-led life to a spirit-led life. Our focus is fixed on the image of Jesus and we are changed into that same image by the Holy Spirit. The changes we experience as we mature spiritually begin with the new birth. His nature is actually placed in us when we believe.

We Must Be Born Again

First we are given the new nature, then the Holy Spirit is given to develop that nature in us. Until we get a new nature from Jesus Christ, there is no spiritual life in us for God to work with.

There is a right way and a wrong way to build a building. God is building us. He wants children that will obey and desire good and not evil. The most important part of a building is the foundation. We cannot erect walls or set a roof in place without first building the foundation. It must be straight, strong and deep enough to support the upper levels.

In my personal life, I knew nothing about the new nature until my sister prayed for me to receive Jesus. After that, things began to happen that could only have been God's intervention. I was born again. One night I had been pondering in my own heart about life and death and about God. I was asking questions in my heart and God was answering them. Suddenly, I realized that God was in the room with me. I felt humbled and could hardly speak. I felt the presence of Jesus right there next to me. I surrendered my life to Him that night and I confessed to Him that I knew that I had failed to make right decisions. I asked Him to please take over my life. That night in a dream Jesus took me to Heaven and I saw my brother who had died in an auto crash. He was fine. I talked with him. Jesus revealed to me that life does not end with death. All the pain of grief left me and peace came into my life for the first time in years. God had already begun healing my heart.

A man named Nicodemus (John 3:3-21 paraphrased) came to Jesus by night to ask him about eternal life. Jesus said, "You must be born again." That confused Nicodemus so he asked. "How can a man go back into his mother's womb and be born again?" Jesus was talking about our spirit which is inside our body. Nicodemus did not yet know that he even had a spirit. Neither do we understand these things until we receive a new nature from Jesus. You see, our very nature, our spirit, has been corrupted by sin and rebellion, causing spiritual death and separation from God. Jesus provided a way, through his own spirit, to get us reconnected with life from God. Jesus died for our sins and rebellion and offers us the opportunity to get back right with God. Then He gives us a brand new spirit from Himself. This is the Gospel. In this scripture, Jesus explained to Nicodemus that which is born of flesh is flesh and that which is born of spirit is spirit. He was saying I will give you a new spirit (a new nature) and restore you to God as a son. John 3:16 says:

For God so loved the world, that he gave his only begotten Son that whosoever believeth in him should not perish, but have everlasting life.

The Son of God came to do what no other man could do. He came to give us a second chance. If you have not yet received Jesus as your Lord to be born again, you can do it right now. Or perhaps you accepted Jesus in your heart but have not really lived the submitted Christian life. This is your opportunity to get back on the path of life and let Him make the changes you need to help you become a son of God. You can pray the simple prayer in the appendix of this book (Appendix A) or pray your own heartfelt prayer and turn your life over to Jesus. He will come to you and you will be saved, washed clean and born again. God loves you no matter what you have done. He will meet you. His love is unconditional. Jesus said, *"Those who come to Me, I will in no wise cast out."* (John 6:37)

The Ministry of the Holy Spirit

The Holy Spirit will teach us truth in the doctrine of Jesus Christ. When Paul got saved, he separated himself for fourteen years until a right foundation was built inside him. He prayed in tongues all those years. Also, Jesus didn't minister in miracles until He was baptized by John and the Holy Spirit in the Jordon river. When we pray in tongues, we are allowing the Holy Spirit to operate and pray through us. The time we give to God, praying in tongues and meditating the Word, is building in us a strong New Testament foundation based on the doctrine of Jesus Christ and not of men. Remember that Paul was not taught in a church but by Jesus Himself.

Now we have the New Testament and Paul's revelations from Christ. We have the doctrine of Jesus Christ: His life and His sayings. Jesus preached to us the Kingdom of God. Our foundation, then, cannot be built on the doctrines of men. Or if we attempt to build our understanding in the Old Testament, we are placing ourselves under the law of condemnation of sin. That covenant is not for followers of Christ; it was for the Jews before Jesus arrived. The Old Covenant has no power to change us, clear our conscience or cleanse us from sin. There is only one way to build a foundation, and it takes spending time with God. We must go deeper into God to get what we need to build a right and strong foundation in Christ.

There are some Christians who went out to win souls for Christ before they went deep enough to get all the truth and they have a weak foundation as a result. God doesn't want us hurt. If God is calling you back to Him for a time, it may be to build in you a stronger foundation, revealing more truth to you so that you will have what you need to finish your course and the calling on your life. We cannot assume that we already have all the truth we need and get complacent. We must separate out time in prayer with God to establish and strengthen ourselves and to hear God. I know that many people do not understand the mysteries hidden in the Gospels. Once the Holy Spirit begins to reveal these truths, your life will be changed forever. You will be amazed at His doctrine, just like the Jews were in Jesus' day.

Jesus spoke in parables and hidden truths in mysteries so that we could search them out with our spirit and discover our great inheritance in Christ. It is all marvelous. He came to reveal the Kingdom of God and the Father to us.

We should covet the gifts of the spirit, especially the gift of personal edification that was given to the Church at Pentecost. The Holy Spirit was sent to empower us for personal change and edification (building up of our new nature). We must be filled as they were in Acts 2:4:

And they were all filled with the Holy Ghost, and began to speak with other tongues, as the Spirit gave them utterance.

The Holy Spirit was working in the Old Testament saints and prophets, but He was not residing INSIDE THEM to empower them to become sons of God. There was no gift of tongues available to them as there is for us now. How shall we refuse God's plan for maturity? We must accept His ways so we can learn and grow. God has provided all we need. I do not want anyone to lose their inheritance as a son of God. Christ died to restore it all to us. I shall not despise His gifts.

The Holy Spirit has been sent to help, comfort, and teach the sons of God. How can He do that if the churches are doing what they want and not giving place for the Holy Spirit to speak? God has things He wants to say to us. Mostly the Holy Spirit cannot speak to the people because the Church has so programmed the service with activities that there is no time or place provided to hear from God Himself. When that happens, a church can become dead in religion. At those times a religious spirit moves in and begins to neutralize the services with formalities and other natural things replacing the voice of God through prophecy and the leadership of the Holy Spirit. Paul set an order in the early churches which allowed the operation and gifts of the Holy Spirit. Paul says of himself that he came with demonstration of power and not with words of man's wisdom. (1 Corinthians 2:2-5)

It has been over 2000 years since Pentecost brought us knowledge of the power of God. We must not allow ignorance of the ministry and gifts of the Spirit to keep us from maturity. These gifts empower the church and also our new nature. It is the work and ministry of the Holy Spirit in our midst that causes us to mature. Jesus said, *"It is expedient (more beneficial) for you that I go away so that the ministry of the Holy Spirit can come to you."* (John 16:7 paraphrased) The gift of tongues (personal edification) is how God communicates with us. The gift of prophecy is how the Holy Spirit speaks to the Church Body.

The Gift of Edification

We are told that the natural man receives not the things of God, for they are foolishness to him. Some people feel foolish when they first begin to pray in tongues. That is our natural man. But inside us is a spiritual man, just like our natural man and it wants to grow and hear God. In 1 Corinthians 2:12-14 Paul explains this:

Now we have received, not the spirit of the world, but the spirit which is of God; that we might know the things that are freely given to us of God. Which things also we speak, not in the words which man's wisdom teacheth, but which the Holy Ghost teacheth; comparing SPIRITUAL THINGS WITH SPIRITUAL. But the natural man receiveth not the things of the Spirit of God: for they are foolishness unto him: neither can he know them, because they are spiritually discerned.

This word tells us that the things of the spirit are spiritually discerned. That means that you cannot understand spiritual things with your carnal mind. Spiritual things can only be received in your newborn spirit. Where is that? you might say. We hear God in the ear of our born-again spirit. I will tell you how I discovered these things, and you can discover for yourself, the voice and power of God in your spirit. If you have difficulty, I recommend to you a free website, (*www.daveroberson.org*) where you can listen to the series "Distinguishing God's Voice." There you can learn how to locate the ear of your spirit and learn from Pastor Dave Roberson where and how exactly you receive God's voice.

At our church, we have set a goal for all believers to be able to hear the voice of God and know without a doubt what God is asking us to do. God wants all His children to know Him and obey Him. It is our delight and pleasure that you understand completely how your spirit operates. It is your inheritance and right as a child of God.

The first instruction my Pastor gave me was to glue myself to a chair and begin praying in tongues. He sent me to the Holy Spirit so I could hear God for myself. I would sit there for hours at a time; weeks even months passed. It was easy, then boring, then hard and it made me very uncomfortable at first. Not anymore. It is a joy and very natural to me now. But when I first began to pray for hours a day, it was unfamiliar and different. The first time I knew something was changing inside of me was because I felt so uncomfortable with myself. In those long hours, I began to confront myself, seeing things I had not seen before. I got so fidgety that I felt I had to quit praying or die. I did die to that flesh part of me and I prayed myself through those times. Finally, I came to a place of peace. At times my mind would wander off, but I would pull it back and begin again, bringing every thought captive and imaginations subject to the obedience of Christ, just by praying in tongues. It's an amazing process.

The very first gift given to the Church was tongues. When we pray in tongues, we allow the Holy Spirit to pray for us in our spirit, and then God answers the prayer. How can we go wrong? We give authority to the prayer as God provides the language. Then He Himself answers our prayer. It is a perfect process of mortification and edification.

Revealing the Mysteries

Through revelation knowledge, we receive understanding of the mysteries hidden in the Word of God. As I continued to use my prayer language, I came to another place of spiritual maturity. Revelation knowledge began to pour into my spirit and suddenly I began to know and understand things I had not known before and I began to identify God's voice inside my spirit.

Pastor Dave told me to read and meditate on only the New Testament. I began praying in the spirit while reading through entire books of the Bible over and over again. I was receiving the scriptural foundation of Christ in my spirit with understanding and within the context of the entire book's message. False religious understanding was being removed from my spirit as I prayed in tongues and true doctrine was being transferred directly into my spirit as I read the Word. I was beginning to understand more fully the doctrine of the Kingdom that Jesus taught, and along with it, my foundation for sonship and inheritance. I was so encouraged when I saw these results.

Power to Heal and Deliver

As I continued praying in tongues, I noticed another change. When I prayed for other people, they got healed and delivered. I was delighted. Power was now operating through my new nature. Depending on what your calling is in the Body, the gifts will be provided by the Holy Spirit to minister that calling to the Body. Evangelists are given miracles; teachers, healing gifts; others are given the word of knowledge, gifts of faith or wisdom to confirm their particular office, administration and operation in the Body of Christ. All these supernatural gifts from God are given to mature us in the leadership of the Holy Spirit in the Church. This is explained in 1 Corinthians, chapter 12.

As I continued praying in the spirit, I learned how to meditate on and assimilate whole books. Now I understand the Born-Again Trail (*www.daveroberson.org*) and the operations of the spirit in the Church. Other scriptures came alive inside me. I was gaining a strong foundation and unshakable belief in Christ and how He operates through the spirit. I felt no more condemnation or guilt for not doing things right. I knew I was free. A foundation was forming in my spirit and I was changing. I was growing and it felt good.

Do Not Give or Take Offenses

Some people are taken out of fellowship with God and the Church by offences. Jesus said offences must come. We must forgive, learn to resist getting offended and be careful with what we say. There is a place in God where things that used to bother us don't bother us anymore. We get there by praying in tongues, which edifies us above the problem. The Holy Spirit protects us in our soul and our emotions. There are many things that can offend us if we get involved on a carnal level. When someone offends us, we can choose to think the best and forgive them, even if they are wrong and we are right. This is operating in agape love. (1 Corinthians 13:5) The more we are perfected in the love of God, the less these carnal things affect us until offences just don't bother us anymore.

When we begin to grow, then the trials will come. Persecution, false accusations, and betrayals will come, many times through those closest to us. Religion and the devil hate it when we grow past these things because we become unmanageable by them and a threat to the devil's kingdom.

When trouble came into my life, I had to hear from God. I needed wisdom. When I thought I was doing well, I fell flat on my face. What was the problem? I had too much flesh. I felt anger and my behavior was awful. I was stumbling all over myself. I needed to put to death my old nature (mortification). I submitted my old nature to the Holy Spirit in prayer, begging for Him to take away what was not pleasing to God.

Mortification of the Old Carnal Nature

Mortification is the same root word as mortician. It means death to the flesh. I found out from the Holy Spirit that if I didn't mortify my old fleshly desires in the same measure that my spirit was growing in power, then the devil could come and use all my weaknesses against me. This is what has stopped revivals and holy men and women in the past.

I found out that my enemy, the devil, uses carefully devised plots and schemes to stop me, kill me or neutralize me over time. But the good news is that his schemes are all based on him using my old flesh nature. He can watch how I react to things because he is a great observer of human nature, but he has no idea what is happening inside me. Remember the Kingdom is inside us. The devil has no access to my born-again spirit. Jesus and I live there. Now that I know what the devil is up to, I can guard myself against his attacks.

Growing up is not always fun, but the reward is great. That is why I want to encourage you to shake off the things of the past and resume your walk in the spirit with Jesus. If we learn to use the POWER God has provided and receive His LOVE, we can get past anything that has stopped us before and go forward in God. He has provided everything for us. He has promised never to abandon us.

To mature is to learn how to receive God's love. God loved us so much that He gave His only Son to save us. God's love is unfathomable. To know God is to love God. God is love. That is His nature. When we are finally perfected in the love of God, there will be no fear. What an awesome power that will be operating in us then. It is the love of God.

Jesus Is Coming for a Bride, Not a Baby

Only after I accepted Jesus into my heart could I even begin to understand God's great love. Things had happened to me in my life that caused me to believe lies about God. I knew how the world operated, but I had no idea how the Kingdom of God operated or the depth of the love of God for us.

Jesus is our First Love. I knew I had committed sins in my life and had done many things wrong. I was so glad to have that load taken off me. I am eternally grateful. What He did for me is so great that I will do anything He asks me to do for Him. However, the process of transformation of my soul was not that easy. My thinking was all messed up. I needed much time in the Word and prayer to straighten it all out. But the Holy Spirit has been faithful to help me change.

Change was much more difficult than I first thought. I had to make many adjustments and I went through some really hard times that first year that I was saved. There were times when I was overwhelmed emotionally. I still remember the confusion, fear, self-doubt and unbelief as I began to come out of my old life and walk in the truth. But I found out through all the trials that God is on my side and He is greater than even my own heart and emotions. He has abundant grace and power available for anyone who is willing to receive them. If we are open to learn, He will teach us. He is our Father and He loves us dearly.

The Word of God Is Our Food for Growth

We cannot grow without nourishment. Our spiritual food is the Word of God: the Bible. If we do not feed our born-again spirit, we cannot grow. We should be reading the Bible regularly.

If the Word has become stale and lifeless, or just "stories," then something is very wrong. There are many preachers today that have something to say. They use the Word to get their message across. They usually collect all the scriptures they need to confirm their message disregarding the context in which the Word is written. They are not hearing the Holy Spirit; they are not rightly dividing the Word. Instead of searching the Word to receive the hidden mysteries they manipulate the Word to deliver *what they want to say*.

These errors occur because of spiritual immaturity and lack of time spent meditating and assimilating the whole passages of truth in context. 2 Timothy 2:15 warns us how to study:

Study to show thyself approved unto God, a workman that needeth not to be ashamed, RIGHTLY DIVIDING the word of truth.

How we receive the Word of God and how we deliver it to other believers is very important to God. We cannot rightly divide the truth until we get the Holy Spirit involved in our meditation of the Word. If we only study as a scholar with our carnal mind, how then shall we receive from the Holy Spirit *what He wrote*? God forbid. Truth comes directly from the Holy Spirit to our spirit *by revelation.* It is given to us by God. It is downloaded directly into our spirit, all at once. Truth is given supernaturally, not naturally. Nothing about God is natural.

When scripture is taken out of its context, people can make it say whatever they want it to say. It is like misquoting another person. We can distort what that person is really saying. Without even realizing it, preachers have done this and created false doctrines by not rightly dividing the Word of God.

Our Diet Is Milk, Then Strong Meat

Milk is the nutrition of a baby. At first that is all we can tolerate. When we are first saved, we are so hungry and desire the milk of the Word. Our nourishment comes from the Word. We learn about faith and grace. When we go to church, we are taught by preachers and teachers the basics of the Christian life. The Holy Spirit, however, is the only One qualified to bring us the truth hidden in the Word. We need Him to show us the hidden mysteries, confirm, enlighten, and reveal truth to us from the Word. Hebrews 5:12-14 says:

For when for the time ye ought to be teachers, ye have need that one teach you again which be the first principles of the oracles of God; and are become such as have need of milk, and not of strong meat. For every one that useth milk is unskillful in the word of righteousness: for he is a babe. But strong meat belongeth to them that are of full age, even those who by reason of use have their senses exercised to discern both good and evil.

Peter talks to his church as a pastor giving advice by the spirit. Peter had learned only to speak what the Holy Spirit gave him to say. In First Peter 2:1-2, Peter tells us how to grow as a baby Christian.

Wherefore laying aside all malice, and all guile, and hypocrisies, and envies, and all evil speakings, as newborn babes, desire the sincere milk of the word that ye may grow thereby:

These scriptures talk about desiring the sincere milk of the Word which are the first principles and oracles of God. He tells us that at this level as babes, we will be experiencing carnality, strife and divisions. We must learn about foundational truths, like repentance, but are not yet ready for a diet of strong meat, where we will learn to discern good from evil so that we are no longer able to be deceived. As we grow and pray in tongues, we will advance to another level, where we will experience the anointing and become more skillful in using the Word and love people, who are God's most precious possession.

In kindergarten, children will play more than learn, and they desire milk. Peter is talking to spiritual babies who want to play as the children of Israel did. Today people want to be entertained, go to casinos, watch movies, and play computer games. Too much worldliness is another reason that many Christians yet remain carnal and spiritual babies. God does not deny us fun, but He does not want us to forsake our Lord and the Kingdom either, leaving off our time in prayer with the Holy Spirit and our communion with Him as our Father. Satan cannot touch our spiritual life but he will use our fleshly desires to lead us away from God, our destiny and inheritance as a son. The more time we spend with God, the more we know Him and the more we defeat the enemy in our lives and family. If we feed our spirit as much as we feed our soul and body, we would be safer from harm from our enemy.

God will come to test our love for Him as we grow. The enemy will also come to tempt us and, if possible, get us off track, stop our spiritual growth or cause us shame and reproach. He wants to rob us of our inheritance in Christ.

Peter loved Jesus so much, but there was something in him that caused him to deny Jesus three times at His trial and crucifixion. Peter was weak and not yet born again. All he had was his old nature. Jesus told Peter, "Satan wants to sift you as wheat, but I have prayed for you that you fail not." As we grow, there are times we are not yet able to do spiritually what we want to do. 1 Corinthians 3:2-3 says:

I have fed you with milk, and not with meat: for hitherto ye were not able to bear it, neither yet now are ye able. For ye are yet carnal: for whereas there is among you envying, and strife, and divisions, are ye not carnal, and walk as men?

Envy, strife and division are some of the things I had in my life. But when I committed to pray in tongues for an allotted period of time each day, the Holy Spirit showed me what was really in my heart. Whatever He is revealing to you is what He wants to change in you. And when you allow Him to do His work in your heart, He will give you the power to change it and will remove it permanently. Only God can do this work. We know from Matthew 19:26 that Jesus knows our weaknesses:

But Jesus beheld them, and said unto them, With men this is impossible; but with God all things are possible.

Whatever the Holy Spirit illuminates in our hearts is the very thing that is keeping us from growing. He admonishes us to look straight ahead, and when He reveals something to us, it is for our good that we attend promptly to this leading of the Holy Spirit. Every time we resort to the arm of the flesh or justify our actions, instead of going to God in prayer, we lose ground spiritually and stop growing. He will wait for us until we obey. The quicker we obey the better. If we wait too long, it can be very difficult to get back on track with God. Obey quickly.

When the spirit showed me strife in my marriage, I had to get rid of it. I didn't know how, but as I yielded over myself for training, meaning praying in tongues, I learned about these things. Each day and in each situation, He revealed more to me about it. I submitted to my Teacher, the Holy Spirit. I could have justified those actions. I could have put blame on my husband. Or I could take personal responsibility, grow up and look to God for wisdom to overcome my weakness. In order to mature as sons of God, we must co-labor together with the Holy Ghost in everything. We can't do this alone, and we can't leave Him out of our daily lives.

Thank God that when we fail and fall, we are still treated with much loving-kindness because *we are God's children.* In the Old Testament, there was more harshness under the Law. Thank God that is no longer the case or none of us would survive. (Adulterers and rebellious children were stoned to death.) Under the Gospel of grace by Jesus Christ, we are given a personal Tutor to lead and guide us into all truth. We are accepted and loved, but still, the Father requires us to change. There is a world to come where no corruption is allowed to enter. We must be perfected here.

Perfecting the New Nature

In Hebrews 5:14, the Word says that mature Christians are those who have their senses exercised to discern good from evil. Adam and Eve had a problem with this. They had an old nature with their soul *ruling* them. They were tempted by their physical senses and fell into the devil's trap. Now we have a new nature, if we are born again, and we have to awaken our spiritual senses to discern good from evil. The Law has been written in our hearts so we know what is right from wrong. However, we have to learn to operate out of our new nature so we are not deceived by our physical senses. Because we are weak we need to build ourselves up in faith, receive the wisdom of God and exercise our spiritual senses to hear God. Then we obey His voice immediately. When we quiet our soul to sit before God, we are exercising our senses to distinguish God's voice from our own soul. Later, I will introduce to you seven spiritual keys to help you exercise your new nature and sharpen your spiritual senses so they become stronger than the carnal senses we used to depend on.

Also, praying in tongues opens the channel from Heaven to receive God's voice. Up until now, our soul has been ruling all our decisions by our five natural senses. The Holy Spirit has been sent to lead and guide us into all truth. Now we must develop the spiritual senses of the new nature in order to hear and see God. We lack much understanding about our new nature and the work of the Holy Spirit in and through us.

The Holy Ghost is the Teacher of our new nature. His job is to bring us to a place of knowing Jesus and the Father as They really are. He will teach us and lead us to the good places of stability, peace and rest. One thing I am learning is to listen carefully to the *inner witness*. That is the most common way that God speaks to us. The Holy Spirit knows me, and when I am about to make a wrong decision, He stops me. I get a "check" inside my spirit to stop and wait. He will also confirm to me the right decisions I make so that there is no doubt what His will is for my life. He leads me out of condemnation and fear into faith and truth. I still make mistakes, but I am learning. The Holy Spirit is like a nurturing Mother who never leaves us and gently guides us into peace. He is the Wisdom to live by that all men look for. He is our private Tutor and more.

In John 1:33, John the Baptist introduces Jesus as the Baptizer of the Holy Spirit.

And I knew him not: but he that sent me to baptize with water, the same said unto me, upon whom thou shalt see the Spirit descending and remaining on him, the same is he which baptizeth with the Holy Ghost.

If you do not yet have the baptism in the Holy Spirit with the evidence of speaking in tongues flowing in your life, please take a moment now to ask Him for this necessary gift. It is from God and it is your inheritance given for your personal growth. Don't let anyone forbid you to have what God has given to you freely at great cost. 1 Corinthians 14:2 says:

For he that speaketh in an unknown tongue speaketh not unto men, but unto God: for no man

understandeth him; howbeit in the spirit he speaketh mysteries.

Some of God's children have stopped growing because they have not yet received their prayer language. I invite you to take a moment to stop here and invite Jesus to baptize you and empower you with your prayer language. *(See Appendix B at end of book)*

God has a plan for our spiritual maturity. He came to us when we were sinners without hope and made us more than conquerors. Now we can be transformed into the image of Jesus Christ, His Son, the perfect Man. But we will need the help of the Holy Spirit to show us how to grow up into sons of God. God is building a spiritual house in us. The baptism and gift of tongues are the foundation for that house. There are yet walls and roof to construct. The doctrine of Jesus is foundational. But first we must receive the Holy Spirit baptism and our spiritual language so God can communicate those mysteries hidden in the Word to us.

Gifts of the Spirit Are Necessary to Mature

Jesus ascended on high to bring us supernatural gifts that will help us mature. These gifts are the power that will bring us together into a unity of faith as one Body. This is how Jesus is building His Church. His goal is oneness in us as in them. (Father, Son and Holy Spirit) Oneness in spirit brings unity and power. One Body and one mind, moving and living in Christ, empowered with gifts and the love of God. In the book of Ephesians, chapter 4, verses 4-16, we can see some of the plan of God to mature us.

There is one body, and one Spirit, even as ye are called in one hope of your calling; One Lord, one faith, one baptism, one God and Father of all, who is above all, and through all, and in you all. But unto every one of us is given grace according to the measure of the gift of Christ. Wherefore he saith, when he ascended up on high, he led captivity captive, and gave gifts unto men. (Now that he ascended, what is it but that he also descended first into the lower parts of the earth? He that descended is the same also that ascended up far above all heavens, that he might fill all things.)

And he gave some apostles; and some, prophets; and some, evangelists; and some, pastors and teachers; For the perfecting of the saints, for the work of the ministry, for the edifying of the body of Christ: Till we all come in the unity of the faith, and of the knowledge of the Son of God, unto a perfect man, unto the measure of the stature of the fullness of Christ: That we henceforth be no more children, tossed to and fro, and carried about with every wind of doctrine, by the sleight of men, and cunning craftiness, whereby they lie in wait to deceive; But speaking the truth in love, may grow up into him in all things, which is the head, even Christ: From whom the whole body fitly joined together and compacted by that which every joint supplieth, according to the effectual working in the measure of every part, maketh increase of the body unto the edifying of itself in love.

The gift of tongues is the first gift we receive to help us mature into sons of God. It is foundational. In this scripture, Paul is asking us to use the gifts of the Holy Spirit that Jesus Christ gave us. God does not want us to be ignorant about the organization of the Church Body and the gifts of the Spirit. The other gifts (nine are mentioned) are given as the Spirit wills. God wants each one of us to be able to do our part to bring the entire Body into maturity and unity of love so He provides what we need to do our part. We need intercession, evangelists, healing gifts, and wisdom from God to bring all the saints to maturity. There is anointing for each calling in the Body of Christ.

Praying in tongues is foundational. It bypasses the mind and intellect. Through the gift of tongues, God has created a way to get truth over to us without our carnal minds distorting it so that we will not fall into deception. Our minds and our enemy, the devil, are great deceivers. The devil also uses religiously trained people, who appear outwardly correct, to take us down a wrong path away from Jesus and the Gospel and into doctrines of men.

Some of those false doctrines are about praying in tongues but we have the Holy Ghost Himself teaching us the doctrine of Jesus from the Word. We do not need to receive doctrines from men. The Word says that tongues are for every believer for *personal edification.* (1 Cor. 14:4) Edify means to build yourself up spiritually. This gift of tongues is absolutely necessary for the gifts and power of God to operate in us. Tongues are not of the devil but directly from the Holy Ghost. In 1 Corinthians 14:18, Paul testifies of this power in his life saying, **I thank my God, I speak with tongues more than ye all.** So then tongues will not make you crazy as some suppose, but will keep you from going crazy if you do as Paul did and pray a lot in the spirit.

This gift of tongues will protect you from false doctrine and you will grow spiritually. When you pray, the Holy Spirit is praying for you. People can teach and we can gain knowledge, but only you can make the decision to take this spiritual journey into God. If somehow I can talk you into giving yourself to praying in tongues, then you will cause the process to begin in your own life. You will start to edify and build yourself up in your inner man through the power of the Holy Spirit and you will mature.

Paul wrote a large portion of the New Testament. He had incredible insight and revelation of the Scripture and words of Jesus. This is the key to why Paul knew so much. He didn't have many books; all he had was *"praying in tongues more than you all."* The supernatural gift of tongues is wisdom from God!

Praying in tongues is the operation of God that brings us into maturity. The Bible says that our carnal mind is enmity against God, and if we lean on our own understanding, we can be led astray because our carnal mind can distort the truth. This language was created by God because there is no language on earth that can totally express what God wants to say. It encompasses all the languages of the world.

Tongues Protects Us from False Doctrine

Beloved, there is only one doctrine that we as Christians should be following. That is the doctrine of Jesus Christ in the Bible, the words of Jesus, and His "sayings." (Luke 6:47-49) This gift will safeguard us from false doctrine if we will just keep praying and don't ever let the devil take us out of prayer.

Whosoever cometh to me and heareth my sayings and doeth them, I will shew you to whom he is like: He is like a man which built an house, and digged deep, and laid the foundation on a rock: and when the flood arose, the stream beat vehemently upon that house, and could not shake it: for it was founded upon

a rock. But he that heareth and doeth not (my sayings) is like a man that without a foundation built an house upon the earth; against which the stream did beat vehemently, and immediately it fell; and the ruin of that house was great.

"Doing His sayings" is priority with Jesus. He made a covenant with us in His own blood. He taught us about where He came from and preached to us how His Father's Kingdom operates. Then Jesus began to teach us *His doctrine.* He did not come to teach us the Law; He came to fulfill the Law by living a righteous life without sin. What He taught us was the Kingdom and how it operates. These are the things we must learn now. We have a new nature and the Holy Spirit to teach us. We can learn these spiritual truths if we follow closely and learn *His way* (Matthew 7:28).

And it came to pass when Jesus had ended these sayings; the people were astonished at his doctrine.

Why were the spiritual leaders of Jesus' time astonished at His doctrine? Perhaps it was because they knew only doctrines taught by men. Jesus was teaching doctrine given to Him by His Father God. He had a personal relationship with the Father. The Pharisees did not know the Father. Even today we must ask ourselves if we believe Jesus' doctrine or what religion from men has taught us. We are now living in the New Covenant in Jesus' blood, not the Old Covenant. We have a better covenant established upon better promises. (Hebrews 8:6)

We Live in the New Covenant, Not the Old.

The Old Testament Law was not cast away. It was fulfilled by Jesus Christ. The condemnation of it was taken to the grave so that we could be made free from guilt forever. The Law was not annulled; it was fulfilled in Jesus Christ. The covenant with God through the blood of animals, however, has now been replaced by a better sacrifice, which is the body and blood of Jesus Christ, who alone is righteous. So now there remains only one covenant, and that is *the blood of Jesus.*

To continue trying to follow God's Old Testament laws is not enough to mature us. There is only one reason for all those laws: to prove to us that we cannot overcome our sinful nature without God's help. Everything we do as born-again Christians must be by grace, from beginning to end. We cannot expect to begin a work of God by the power of His spirit, and then complete it by our own power without Him. We need the help of the Holy Spirit and the nature of Jesus on the inside of us. Jesus has already overcome the things we will face in life.

Our Spirit Is Now Alive. Jesus' DNA Is in Us.

The Holy Spirit begins His work in our new nature. Jesus had the DNA of Mary but also DNA from His Father God in Heaven. Jesus' nature in us is spirit and able to receive spiritual things. We were all dead in our spirit until we accepted Jesus and His life came into us and made us alive. He quickened us. In Romans, chapter 8, verse 29, Jesus reveals Himself as the *Firstborn of many brethren* (a new species).

For whom he did foreknow, he also did predestinate to be conformed to the image of his Son, that he might be the *firstborn among many brethren.*

DNA is the microscopic material that contains the image in the seed of life. It is the programming for every living creature. It is the material of creation. God created a woman out of the DNA of Adam while he slept. Science teaches the model to us in biology class in high school. The rib that the scripture refers to in Genesis 2:22 reveal God's creative reproduction on a microscopic level. God changed one sex chromosome in the strand of DNA from Adam to create Eve who is the female of that species. In the same manner that God created woman out of Adam's DNA, God also created the sons of God out of Jesus' DNA. The blood of Jesus provided the DNA. It is all very legal and scientific. The model for the born-again man is revealed throughout the New Testament. I don't have time to go into that here but it is the Gospel. Jesus reveals His plan for us to become sons of God after His true identity (DNA) in John 12:24:

Verily, verily, I say unto you, except a corn of wheat fall into the ground and die, it abideth alone: but if it die, it bringeth forth much fruit.

Jesus died and presented His blood to the Father in Heaven. That blood contained the DNA of a new creature. Jesus is a Man who was dead and is now alive and glorified in a new body. That model is what we become when we accept Jesus' plan of salvation. In this scripture, Jesus is telling us that when He dies, there will be more sons of God created after His image. They will have His nature as a son of God and be trained up by the Holy Spirit. They will function as Jesus did, in the power of God, wisdom of God and the love of God. To produce more sons like Jesus, God the Father needed to give us a new nature with the ability to be molded into a son of God. Someone righteous had to be willing to sacrifice His life to produce more sons after His kind. That someone was Jesus. He alone could do this job.

Can you picture a strand of DNA intertwined with the spirit of God? Jesus' blood carried the DNA of God and man, thereby creating a new species, which we call the born-again man. When we are saved, we receive the very nature of Christ and the eternal life that is in Him. Jesus is the God-Man Glorified. He is the righteousness of God in a flesh body. We are now able to conform to His image because we have His nature inside us. Now the Holy Spirit has something to work with, and He is able to perform that work of spiritual maturity in us.

We Mature by Faith

Maturity comes by believing. It takes faith. There was a covenant made between God and Abraham. Abraham wanted children and so did God. Now this is only an imagined scene based on scripture but a dialogue between God and Abraham might have gone something like this:

"Tell me Abraham, will you offer up your only son as a sacrifice to me? And do you believe I can raise up a new heir for you from the dead?" Abraham believed God and God replied *"OK then, I will not require your son Isaac, but I will give up my son Jesus to die instead and He will become the firstborn of a new species that will restore all mankind to righteousness. Do you believe in my plan Abraham?"*

Jesus came, *died* and was glorified in His body. We believe by faith that we shall also rise from the dead and be glorified. When we believe, we become sons of God with His nature. Jesus set the pattern. He became the firstborn of many brethren. (Romans 8:29) The Father wanted many sons. Because Abraham believed and now we believe, we can be those sons. Understanding like this comes to us more clearly as we assimilate more of the New Testament. The Holy Spirit will correct false doctrine and replace it with truth from the Word as we pray in tongues.

Romans 6:14 tells us that sin shall not have dominion over us. That is true because we have the nature of Christ in us now and it is righteous. We are no longer just sinners (with an old nature) saved by grace, we are sons of God (with a new nature). We can receive our inheritance as God's sons. We receive the ability to obey God's commandments as Jesus did because we have God's very nature. We just need the training of the Holy Ghost to mature us in that new nature. When we receive the baptism in the Holy Ghost with evidence of speaking in tongues, the Holy Spirit helps us to walk in God's Ways. So we can conclude that our spirit is eternal and righteous and our bodies will be changed. Maturity is on the way as we press into God and allow the Holy Spirit to lead and guide us into all truth.

It is a process to grow up, transform, renew our minds, and mature into the sonship of God and it doesn't happen overnight. We must put off the old nature habits and put on the new nature of God as we learn to live like Jesus did as sons of God.

Mysteries are revealed by Praying in Tongues

Understanding the Word of God and the mysteries hidden in it are vital to our maturity. We can get the Holy Ghost involved in our meditation and assimilation of the word when we pray in tongues while reading through the books of the New Testament.

Many people say that they don't understand the Bible. The Holy Spirit was sent to reveal the mysteries hidden in Jesus' words from the Father. These very mysteries can set us free from wrong thinking, errors and false doctrine. The hidden understanding in these verses will open up the entire message around it. This requires us to take time alone with the Holy Spirit and the Word. We must give Him what He needs to bring us into maturity.

I encourage you to give the Holy Spirit time in the prayer closet to do this precious work of revelation knowledge, personal edification and transformation in your life. There is an inner work that God wants to do in each of us. An ear of corn has to grow and develop on the *inside* first. (Mark 4:28) The time you spend allowing the Holy Spirit to develop your new nature in God will produce the most valuable fruit of your life. This is where godly change and growth come from.

Religion Will Be Replaced by Truth

Jesus loves the Bride, His Church, but somewhere along the way, religion and ego began to creep into the Chruch and along with it, false doctrines of every sort. Then, leaders who were trained up under these false doctrines began to teach others, propagating more false doctrine. Some have proclaimed allegiance to those doctrines not even realizing that they are teaching other people's false doctrine.

Most often talented men will follow religious doctrines of men to build their own empire and then they continue in it because the glory and admiration of success is addicting. These people do not have our personal growth in mind. They have other motives. They will use *"sleight of men and cunning craftiness"* (Ephesians 4:14) to deceive. What this does is it causes people to look at them striking a dependency on them instead of leading us to depend on God; the Holy Spirit. They then use this dependency to control believers creating a prison for them. This is religion and unfortunately, this has been the way of some of the churches. The Bible instructs church leaders to be servants to the body in their particular gifts and callings. (Mark 10:44) There is respect but not control. It is our job to point people to Jesus, not ourselves. May God forgive us and help us to correct this before Jesus returns.

Now that I have discovered the ministry and leadership of the Holy Spirit in my life, I find that the Holy Spirit is much more qualified to lead me into all truth. My goal now is to help others strike a dependence on Jesus and the Holy Spirit and to empower every believer. Praying in tongues does this. It puts the Holy Spirit in charge of our life. The Holy Spirit is faithful to help us remove all religion, false doctrine, sin and control.

In the soul of the unregenerate man is that desire for admiration from men. What we need is God's nature *and* the Holy Spirit training us up as sons to get free from our old nature ego and develop our new nature in Christ. Jesus spoke to the religious leaders about these very things in John 5:39-44:

Search the scriptures: for in them ye think ye have eternal life and they are they which testify of me. And ye will not come to me, that ye might have life. I receive not honour from men. But I know you that ye have not the love of God in you, I am come in my Father's name, and ye receive me not; if another shall

come in his own name, him ye will receive. How can you believe who receive honour one from another and seek not the honour that comes from God only?

Jesus equates this desire for recognition with unbelief. How can you believe if you receive honor from men and not from God? This is a key to holiness and giving all the glory to God.

We all come to Jesus from a different path but we are all going to the same place. I was raised Catholic, then Baptist, then Pentecostal. I had to be purged from wrong doctrine that I had received from all these churches. I have learned to never take what men say as truth. I must get confirmation from the Word. We should be taking everything we hear to Jesus in prayer, looking to the Word of God and the Holy Spirit to reveal the truth to us. (John 2:24-25)

But Jesus did not commit himself unto them because he knew all men. And needed not that any should testify of man; for he knew what was in man.

Meeting with God in our Private Prayer Time

In this journey to spiritual maturity it is critical to keep a steady prayer life. There are tools available to help us do this so we won't fall back into old patterns of religion or flesh that used to rule our soul. Jesus would separate out for himself prayer time even in the midst of multitudes pressing upon him. He maintained daily communion with the Father and the Holy Spirit, sometimes He prayed all night.

The first impasse we encounter as we begin to pray in tongues is to not be taken out of prayer. If you don't stop praying, you WILL get victory every time. God will come but the devil will come first with distractions of every kind, things to do, worries, emotions using circumstances and people, even family to draw you out of prayer. When you are not praying, you are not growing and you get weaker spiritually. That is why we must develop this discipline in holy stubbornness to endure these assaults of the enemy against our soul. Once the devil is convinced he can't steal your prayer time with God, He will leave off pursuing you in this way. This is a battle you must win.

Meeting with God to get His instructions for the day and maintaining a close personal walk will keep you strong spiritually and the enemy will have no place in you. I am a morning person so I get up early. Usually the Lord is waiting for me. I get out my red book, the bible and my journal to take notes. My red book is a collection of personal notes, prophecies and confessions that God has given me to help guide me into His presence and His will for the day. It is my life in God. It contains sections on direction, personal prophecies, private worship, confessions, and meditation of the word.

I begin worshipping the Lord and as He speaks I write down what he is saying. I ask Him questions and He answers them. He leads me to whatever section I need that day and I confess His word over whatever is still in unbelief. If I am asking for power or a gift of the spirit He will tell me what is required to operate in that and I confess the word over it. When my day begins I am ready. I know His will.

Seven Spiritual Keys

There are seven very important spiritual keys that we at the Prayer Center use to help guide us in our prayer time with God. These are areas of spiritual growth that the Holy Spirit has given us to keep us on the path and out of deception. Incorporating these keys in your life will unlock doors into the higher levels of spiritual growth.

Meditate, pray and focus on what God has for your life, especially over the prophecies you've received. Prophecies are markers in your path. The Holy Spirit will direct your every step and alert you to any upcoming attack of the enemy. Prepare yourself for the day by "checking in", allowing the Lord time to speak to you. Be thankful and encourage yourself by calling to remembrance all that He is doing and has done for you. The Holy Spirit will direct you on how and when to use these keys to build up your spirit. The devil has no place here. This is kingdom business and God's workmanship.

1. **<u>Praying in the spirit</u>** (tongues) is that supernatural language that was given to us when we were baptized by Jesus in Holy Spirit. This is the gift of revelation and power to communicate with God where truth is revealed to us. This is what separates those who walk in power from those who do not. This is our spiritual language used for personal edification and it is for every believer. It is private between you and God. There are other diversities of tongues that I will not talk about here.

2. **Meditation and assimilation of the Word**. In this method, a believer will learn to meditate day and night as described in Psalm One. Meditation is not bible study nor is it memorizing the scripture. When we read the Word of God while praying in tongues, the Holy Spirit can transfer revelation knowledge to our born again spirit. It is important to read the bible in whole sections asking the Holy Spirit where to begin and end the reading so that we won't take any verses out of context. In this manner, one can receive a full picture from the mind of Christ directly into our spirit, all at once. God actually transfers understanding of the mysteries and revelation knowledge directly to us from the mind of Christ.

3. **Private worship.** God seeks true worshippers who worship in spirit and in truth. A daily practice of private worship brings great fruit in our lives. Knowing God intimately is our goal. Worship is learned as we offer ourselves to Him as a sacrifice at first, then in great anticipation of His loving presence. Our heavenly Father seeks believers who operate in New Testament truth from their spirit. God responds to our worship with favor and presence. He woos and draws us into intimacy with Himself. The more time we spend with Him in worship the more we know Him as our Father.

4. **Confession of His word**. Confession is an operation of faith that brings us from unbelief into believing what God has said. By faith we take hold of his promises and grow. As we confess His word back to Him, our soul and mind are transformed into perfect agreement with truth as He has spoken it. I take scriptures and personalize

them and repeat them to myself until I believe them. I say it to myself many different ways to convince my own soul.

5. **Fasting**. Fasting helps us to put to death the motives that rule our old nature of sin. It allows us to see more clearly the roots of the strongholds that have ruled in our soul. The Holy Spirit helps us destroy all the works the enemy has planted in our lives, leaving us in peace without torments and fears. Fasting, with prayer can defeat deeply rooted things out of our flesh nature. Until we get our glorified bodies, we will have to deal with our carnal nature with its lusts and desires.

6. **Sitting before God.** We must learn how to quiet our spirit in order to hear the voice of God speak to us. We can shut down the operation of the flesh to hear His voice. God is always with us but we can occupy our minds with busy activities, worries and cares. We fall into error when we act on our own, thinking it is God when it is not. Usually it is our soul. Many times I thought I heard from God but I was in error because I did not wait on God. We must not move out until we have peace inside.

7. **Practicing the presence of God.** We have to learn how to walk by the leading of the Holy Spirit, find the ear of the spirit, hear and obey His voice alone. We must trust God to provide the wisdom to walk us out of our old self into everything God wants us to be. Our Comforter wants to teach us all these things and more.

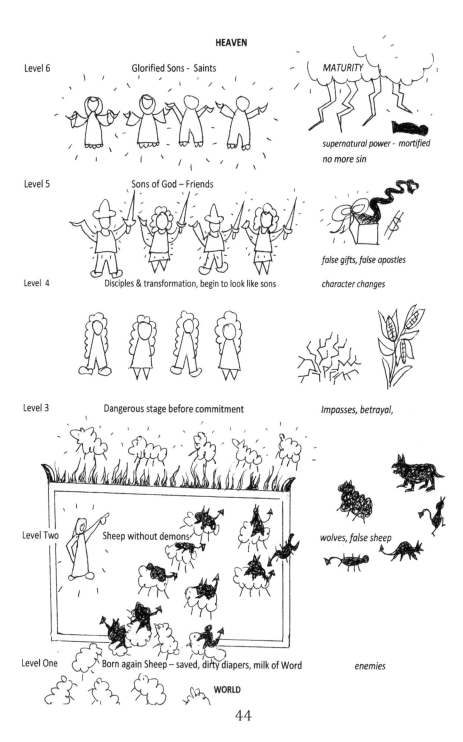

Six Levels of Spiritual Maturity

In this book, I am presenting to you an overview of spiritual maturity as God has revealed it to me in six levels. There are many levels, but for teaching purposes I'm using only six. As we grow into these levels, we bring glory to Jesus and to the Father. He delights in us when we come into a walk of power and obedience in the works of God. Let this book serve as a guide to help you see your personal spiritual growth and to encourage yourself as you learn new things about the Kingdom and your Father.

The Father, Son and Holy Spirit are each involved in our spiritual growth. The Father prunes and corrects. The Son Jesus is our example of what a son of God ought to be like. He is also the Word and Head of the body. He gave us our new nature and we are made in His image. His work on earth is done and He now sits in heaven ruling after the power of an endless life as our high priest and intercessor. The things He encountered among men, we will also encounter. The Holy Spirit is our Helper, nurturer, Comforter and private tutor.

Our Father is concerned with every aspect of our spiritual growth and is intimately involved at every level. He is a good Father and gives only good gifts. (Mt. 7:11) He loves you and always has your best interests at heart. We should respect Him but not be afraid to ask Him for our needs. He is our provider. Only a true son will receive correction from his Father. Your Father is pleased with every effort you make to mature.

Jesus is the builder. Jesus' word is the building material God uses to build our house. We are His workmanship. Philippians 1:6 tells us that Jesus began a good work in us that he is well able to complete.

The Holy Spirit delivers God's gifts, work and power directly into our spirit. When you connect with the Holy Spirit as your teacher, He will lead and guide you into all truth and reveal all things to you. Ask God for a teachable spirit to receive all He has to give you. Then just get yourself into position to receive what the Holy Spirit is giving and put it into practice as He speaks. God wants you to know what He is doing with you. He wants you to understand Him and know Him. He will help you and encourage you when you need it. He knows what your limits are and what your calling and purpose in life is.

The righteous shall live by faith. Faith alone pleases God. We must learn to trust God's work in us. Living by faith and trusting in God is against our old nature but we must learn how and not think that we can do things in our own effort without Him. His work is supernatural and good. We are new creatures now. As we grow, we will bear fruit for God. Our fruit will be love, peace, joy and other characteristics that reflect his character of love and in John 15:16 Jesus says,

You have not chosen me, but I have chosen you, and ordained you, that you should go and bring forth fruit, and that your fruit should remain: that whatsoever ye shall ask of the Father in my name, he may give it you.

We also need the grace that Jesus provides to walk out the plan of God for our lives. Jesus' faith was tested along the way as we also will be. He learned how to walk in faith and grace. All these tests of faith will make us stronger. Because Jesus passed His test, He has made His ability available to us by substitution. He will trade our weaknesses for His faith to get us through any trial.

As our spiritual eyes mature, we begin to see Jesus as He is and ourselves as sons of God. This comes about as we grow. Since we are born blind to spiritual things, we need to develop eyes of faith to see as God sees. Confession of the word will begin to open the eyes of our understanding to know how God sees us. We choose to leave off our blindness and old ways. The things that seem so impossible for us now will become reality later on as we walk in faith believing. It is only when we stop praying and believing that we stop growing.

The entire process of maturity entails leaving off the old flesh nature ruled by our soul and moving into a life led by the Spirit in our new nature. Our final goal is to become like our Lord who walked out His calling with compassion, power and truth in love. Spiritual maturity in 1 John 2:5-6 means that we should walk as Jesus walked.

But whoso keepeth His word, in Him verily is the love of God perfected: hereby know we that we are in Him. He that saith he abideth in Him ought himself also so to walk, even as He walked.

Jesus, the Father and the Holy Spirit are working to perfect you every day. We are God's workmanship. Jesus gave us parables to explain how our Father works in our lives to prune back the wild branches to make us fruitful.

A parable is a natural example of a spiritual truth. Jesus teaches us by example these spiritual truths so that we can understand the kingdom and how God operates in us. Jesus is a great teacher.

A Wild Olive Tree Engrafted into Natural

I am the true vine, and my Father is the husbandman, every branch in me that beareth no fruit He taketh away; and every branch that beareth fruit, He purgeth it, that it may bring forth more fruit. Now you are clean through the word I have spoken unto you, abide in me, and I in you. As the branch cannot bear fruit of itself, except it abide in the vine; no more can ye, except ye abide in me. I am the vine, ye are the branches: he that abideth in me, and I in him, the same bringeth forth much fruit: for without me you can do nothing.

Jesus compares us to trees or vines in his Father's vineyard in John 15:1-6. In our spiritual growth, the Father will come at times and seasons in our lives to "prune" us. The enemy also comes to attack us even at these same times. There are also storms and circumstances that occur, but the tree is expected to grow strong, endure the storms of life and bear fruit for the master as we continue in prayer in Him.

When I was young, I was full of ambition to make myself look good. I wrote out resumes to present myself a little bit better than I really was. I showed only the good points and left out the weaknesses. I learned the world's ways.

I didn't realize it then, but my life was full of corrupt ways of the world and there were many things God wanted to correct. God saw that I needed to be purged from these things. I was superficial in agape love and worship. I was religious and controlled by fears and lusts. I was ambitious thinking mostly of myself. I got angry, offended easily, envy and jealousy rose up inside my thoughts and heart. The trials and pruning of the Father began to chop off those wild limbs and I was cut back severely.

Then the enemy came in with condemnation, oppression, depression, false accusations came from people, judgments and criticism. I was being humbled. Do you remember the story of Job who lost everything? I had to learn like Job, that everything I had was from God's favor on my life, it was not my own abilities that gained me success, it was right living and favor from a righteous God.

As I reflect back on my own spiritual growth, I can see that I was as a wild vine. I can see the work of the Holy Spirit. The Father came to prune my branches and the Holy Spirit began to lead me into a greater intimacy and knowledge of God. Now as I look back, I can see the good fruit that was produced because my Father came and pruned back those wild branches growing in me. Can you see the progression of maturity from a wild vine to a fruit bearing vine?

A Pruned Tree Bears Good Fruit.

Wild branches	Pruned branches	Fruit bearing
Music Sunday only and music of world	Vain words of religious show	Sincere adoration & worship
Religious duty without fasting	Dead religion	Fasted life, obedience
Ashamed and condemned	Acceptance, without condemnation	Wisdom and boldness to testify
Unrighteousness	Self righteousness	Jesus' righteousness
Lusts of eyes-self prosperity, cravings	Giving under law & tithe	Kingdom giving
Self-effort, works My way	rebellion	Holiness Surrender
Hatred, strife, envy, jealousy, lies, bitterness	Gifts without love, lying character flaw	Power of God Temperance change
No fruit, easily offended unteachable spirit	First fruits Deeper roots	Resurrection life, love, maturity
Pride, self-exaltation	Humiliation	Servant's heart and obedience

Level One - Born Again with a New Nature

Jesus came for me when I was in a very pitiful state and because my sister had been praying for me. He saves us because He loves us. I used to feel so condemned for my sinful ways but now I know that He loves me and came to help me. His priority was to save me. He didn't expect me to change that day. But He did give me a new nature. Later, when I was more able to endure it, change came into my life. I knew that no change was possible without God's help. Jesus sent the Helper, the Holy Spirit; to help me make the changes I desperately needed.

Jesus wants us to bring our brothers and sisters back to the Father. All people have a sin nature and need a new nature from Christ. The sons of God are not converting people to religion or a philosophy like Islam or Buddhism; instead we are bringing people out of the control of the devil and a nature of sin into safety with Jesus who loves them and died for them. Jesus is the Savior. There is pure joy, no sorrow or bondage in Christ. Christianity is voluntary, not imposed. The world needs a Savior, not more law or religion. The law could not save anybody. Jesus saves everyone. Salvation in Christ is not based on our merit or works; it is based on His work and His sacrifice. It is a finished work and a perfect work accepted by God the Father as explained in John 1:11-13.

He came unto His own (Jews) and His own received him not. But as many as received Him, to them gave He power to become the sons of God, even to them that believe on His name: which were born, not of

blood, nor of the will of flesh, nor of the will of man, but of God.

Jesus came to me because it was His will. He loved me. He will give each of us the power to mature as sons of God. He did not do all the work for us but he gave us the absolute ability to be made righteous. Then as we grow and learn to obey God, we learn to yield to the voice of the Holy Spirit and Jesus, the Word.

Co-laboring with the Holy Spirit enables us to grow. Jesus never intended to leave us alone as orphans after we were saved. He didn't just send us an angel, He sent us the Holy Spirit himself. Together we will experience every level of growth into sonship. We are never alone, no matter how we feel. With the help of the Holy Spirit and the careful pruning of the Father, we overcome every attack of the enemy. We no longer have to be ruled by the weak nature of flesh, now we can learn to walk with God. We also have access to the power and wisdom of God.

We give God great joy as we spend more time in fellowship with Him. *Worship* brings us into His presence and also brings healing to our wounded soul. As we mature we are made whole. When we begin to come out from the world and Satan's influence into God's presence, God teaches us many things about the kingdom of God.

Big S and little s Communicate

In Romans chapter eight, I discovered the operation of the Holy Spirit (big S) as He communicates with our new nature (little s). I had been confused about the word spirit in that chapter. Which spirit is He talking about? Then I decided to meditate and assimilate that chapter until I understood who was talking to whom? Pastor Dave Roberson had been preaching from that chapter and I did not understand it.

Pastor explained that In the Greek language there is only one word for "spirit", so in English it is left up to the translators to decide which spirit is referred to. The only way to distinguish between the word "spirit" (referring to the new nature we receive from Christ) and "Spirit" (which refers to the third person of the Godhead, the Holy Spirit) is by understanding its context and how it is used.

Beginning in Romans chapter eight, verses 1-15 the word spirit (little s) refers to our born again spirit or new nature given us from Jesus Christ. It is not until verse 16, where it says the "Spirit itself", do we see the Holy Spirit introduced. This is important for us to know because this chapter explains *how* the Holy Spirit communicates with our new nature and *how* the Holy Spirit interacts with our born again spirit. I encourage you to meditate and assimilate this chapter first. It is foundational, the center and pivotal chapter of the New Testament.

Many people have confused the work of Holy Spirit with our new nature. Some believe that the Holy Spirit is somehow doing everything and we are to do nothing. This is so wrong. **Unless we do what the Holy Spirit is directing us to do, we will not get past ourselves.** It is our authority in the new nature that God uses. We are a team as much as Jesus and the Holy Spirit were when He walked in the earth. We must cooperate with the Holy Spirit also by doing our part in this maturity process.

When we receive our spiritual language, we cooperate by moving our lips and making sounds with our voice. The Holy Spirit delivers the prayer to our spirit man but we must speak it out. God works with us. We cannot allow ourselves to get too proud either. We can do nothing without God and He won't do anything more with us until we obey what He has already asked us to do. It is truly a partnership with God. We must do everything together.

Our New Nature enables us to Hear God

The only channel through which we can hear God is through our spirit. We develop our spiritual hearing as we pray in tongues. Some people have not yet developed the ear of their spirit and much of what they hear is from their soul and their emotions. We can fall into many traps and errors if we have not yet learned to discern the voice of God in our spirit. Here is an exercise that can help. Pray in tongues for about twenty minutes then stop and listen inside. You will hear the tongues continue inside and that is the place where the ear of your spirit is located. Listen there for God's voice.

The Holy Ghost wants to speak to us. Just as we learn to talk in our native tongue, we learn by speaking out those sounds more and more using our spiritual language. The communication line from the Holy Spirit opens up when you pray in tongues and spiritual messages can be revealed to your spirit. This process will make more and more sense as you use your spiritual language and seek the Holy Spirit. We had become accustomed to taking orders and direction from our soul instead of our spirit. Now we must restrain our soul in order to follow God's voice. There is a reordering inside us that must take place. When we mature in hearing God we will no longer be babes tossed to and fro by every wind of doctrine. (Ephesians 4:14)

When I got saved, *life* came into my dead spirit and made me alive for the first time. All the weight of sin and failure came off of my shoulders and I was forgiven. But because all I knew was works, being raised a Catholic, I quickly took up burdens again and became weighed down. The Holy Spirit showed me what I was doing and now I am aware of that weakness so I guard myself against stepping out ahead of God. I am learning to wait for confirmation from the Holy Ghost.

As babies using our new language, we are not yet able to understand and digest the meat (mysteries) of the Word. We also have a lot of baggage from the world and religion. Our Father loves us and receives us as His own but there is much the Holy Spirit desires to teach us about the kingdom of God. Jesus knew when He left this world that we would need a Helper and Comforter in our journey into spiritual maturity. In order to mature as Christians we also need constant edification to build ourselves up above our sensual flesh nature, on our most holy faith. (Jude 18-21) This is the major reason why we pray in tongues, in the Holy Spirit.

On the day of Pentecost a mighty rushing wind came where the 120 were gathered together. The Holy Ghost had arrived on earth to begin his ministry. He is our Helper, Comforter, Finger of God, Spirit of Truth, Wisdom of God and much more. In the New Testament He is the power given to us to mature us, train us, and instruct us in God's ways. He gives gifts to empower us to do the work Jesus has called us to do. Basically, the Holy Spirit enables us to walk in the supernatural things of God.

Level Two - Authority over Devils

At this level we discover that there are demons attached to the sheep. We did not realize it nor could we see into the spirit world until we were born again. Now we begin to discern more of what is good and what is evil but we are still sensual beings ruled by our five natural senses. This makes us vulnerable to the influence of evil spirits, demons and wolves. Jesus tells us about the spirit world and gives us power over evil spirits as sons of God. Deliverance and healing are some of the things we learn about as we grow up into spiritual things. In Mark 6: 7-10, Jesus instructs His disciples before He sends them out. On their return they were amazed that they had power over unclean spirits (devils).

And He called unto him the twelve, and began to send them forth two by two; and gave them power over unclean spirits; and commanded them that they should take nothing for their journey, save a staff only; no scrip, no bread, no money in their purse; but be shod with sandals; and not put on two coats, and He said unto them, in what place soever ye enter into an house, there abide till ye depart from that place.

In our walk with Jesus, at this level of maturity we may begin to realize that there are many devils in the world and in our lives. We now have the opportunity to make a decision to rid ourselves of these evil influences. We are learning about the enemies of God and the Kingdom of darkness.

Looking at the illustration again at level two I have begun a new column of drawings on the right side of the page. Simultaneously with our spiritual growth are the *attacks of Satan* attempting to stop us at each level. We have enemies but remember they are spiritual enemies, not people. Here we learn about satan's tactics and we learn how to fight *a spiritual warfare.* But we must be careful never to hurt a little one in the process. The enemy is a liar and a deceiver and he is very good at it. He can put disease on our bodies and bring many evil things against us. His goal is threefold: Satan comes to steal, kill and destroy. He doesn't do anything else, He doesn't know anything else. He is a murderer, liar and a thief. (John 10:10)

The thief cometh not, but for to steal, and to kill, and to destroy: I am come that they might have life, and that they might have it more abundantly.

We must not give place to the devil and we do have authority over him. As we mature we learn how to deal with our flesh nature, the devil and with God's chastening. We will grow and if we don't quit allowing the Holy Spirit access in prayer to teach us, we will get home safely to the Father and finish our course here on earth.

The Christian walk is simple but it is not easy. We must believe in our heart, confess God and renounce the devil. There is also another enemy we must overcome at the same time and that is the evil nature inside us. So the battle then is mostly inside us, not outside us as some would have us believe. Jesus says this in Mark 7:15, and 21-23:

There is nothing from without a man, that entering into him can defile him: but the things which come out of him those are they that defile the man. For from within, out of the heart of men, proceed evil thoughts...and defile the man.

At level two, we learn to discern what comes from our old nature and what comes from the devil. God is also there instructing and correcting us. How can we know these things if we do not co-labor with the Holy Spirit and get Him involved? Therefore, I submit that tongues is a very necessary part of our spiritual maturity and we simply cannot do without it if we are going to win our spiritual battles.

The Holy Spirit speaking into our spirit will lead and guide us into all truth. He is the one who will show us all things and bring the Word to our remembrance. How important it is to keep praying in tongues as we go through this process of transformation and maturity into our inheritance as sons. We begin to realize now that we will certainly need the Helper, there is no other way! That is why Jesus says in John 16:13-14:

Howbeit when He, the Spirit of truth is come He will guide you into all truth for He shall not speak of Himself: but whatsoever He shall hear that shall He speak: and He will show you things to come. He shall glorify me; for He shall receive of mine, and shall show it unto you.

Level Three - No Turning Back

This is a time of commitment when we declare our choice and decision to follow God and His plan for our life. We are not yet free of all demonic influences neither are we free of our old nature of flesh and sin. The enemy lurks at every level of spiritual growth. Even though things may appear quiet for a time, the enemy is observing us constantly to find weaknesses in our flesh where he can stop us in our pursuit of God and keep us from going any further into God. He would like to get you to stop receiving from the Holy Spirit. He would like to convince you to quit that incessant praying in tongues. This is because he is afraid of you growing up.

If you should get past your weaknesses by the power of God, then he is finished. He knows you have more power *in Christ* than he does as prince of this world. Now the devil changes his tactics. He will try to keep us operating in the flesh (temptations) and attempt to convince us not to make a commitment to walk in power as sons of God. Ultimately the enemy wants to keep us from receiving our inheritance from Christ. Have you stopped at this level of spiritual growth? If so, just start up again. It's not over until it's over.

Learn How to Handle Betrayal

It stands to reason that if we are going to commit ourselves to walking in the spirit, then the enemy will send those close to us to betray us. This is another strategy the enemy uses to stop us at this level. But God is using these attacks of betrayal to teach us how to handle betrayal as sons. The love of God is being perfected in us as we learn to pray for our enemies and wash the feet of the betrayer as Jesus did with Judas before His betrayal. These are lessons of love we shall never forget and neither does God the Father forget. Vengeance belongs to God, not us. Here I learned that the more I die to self, the more power comes into my life.

In the illustration I have depicted flames and also curved objects at the upper corners of the sheep pen. These are similar to the horns of the altar that the Old Testament priests used to tie the animals to the altar when they were slain for sacrifice. Our flesh will squirm and try to get out from under the death of our flesh. When it comes to dying to self, the flesh wants out. The brazen altar is a type and shadow of that place of sacrifice where the innocent lamb is slain. As we give up being led by the soul we begin to be led by the spirit. Our surrender produces the spirit of holiness.

This death to self is called *mortification.* We cannot grow in our old nature, it has been declared dead by God. So now our new nature will spring forward as the soul (mind, will and emotions) surrenders its rule over us.

Decide to be Teachable

The day you decide to sit before the Teacher in the classroom of the Holy Spirit is the day you begin your transformation and spiritual walk into the power of God. Praying in tongues and sitting before God for extended periods of time will give the Holy Spirit access to your born-again spirit to clean up your heart and spirit so He can put your life in order as a son of God.

Praying for hours doesn't feel good. It is a decision to put God first. Remember, when you pray in tongues for extended periods of time you are giving Him permission *to pray for you.* He does not use your carnal mind. You can rest, worship or meditate and assimilate books of the Bible. If your mind wanders, bring it back and begin again. But continue to move your lips and pray giving your heart over to the Holy Ghost for his supernatural work of transformation inside you. Read Romans 8:7-11 below.

Because the carnal mind is enmity against God; for it is not subject to the law of God, neither indeed can be. So they that are in the flesh cannot please God. But you are not in the flesh, but in the spirit (new nature being developed in you) if so be that the spirit of God dwell in you. Now if any man has not the spirit of Christ, he is none of his. And if Christ be in you, the body is dead because of sin; but the spirit is life because of righteousness.

We submit to the Teacher giving over rule by our own soul on purpose, as this verse explains in Ephesians 4:20-24:

But ye have not so learned Christ; if so be that ye have heard Him and have been taught by Him, as the truth is in Jesus: that ye put off concerning the former conversation the old man, which is corrupt according to the deceitful lusts' and be renewed in the spirit of your mind: and that ye put on the new man, which after God is created in righteousness and true holiness.

The Holy Spirit receives the words of Jesus from the throne and communicates to our born again spirit. As we pray in tongues He is receiving instructions and prayers from Jesus *our intercessor* and delivers them to our spirit, then we pray it out of our mouth in tongues. He is helping us put off the old and put on the new, working in us the transformation from sheep to servants and from servants to sons as we yield ourselves over to His wisdom and grace. Colossians 3:8-15 reveals this process:

But now we also put off all these: anger, wrath, malice, blasphemy, filthy communication out of your mouth. Lie not one to another, seeing that ye have put off the old man with his deeds; and have put on the new man which is renewed in knowledge after the image of him that created him: where there is neither Greek nor Jew, circumcision nor uncircumcision, Barbarian, Scythian, bond nor free: but Christ is all, and in all. Put on therefore, as the elect of God, holy and beloved, bowels of mercies, kindness, humbleness of mind, meekness, longsuffering; forbearing one another and forgiving one another, if any man have a quarrel against any; even as Christ forgave you, so also do ye. And above all these things, put on (love), which is the bond of perfectness. And let the peace of God rule in your hearts and be ye thankful.

Here, the Holy Spirit gives us specific details about our transformation process out of the old nature of flesh and into the new image as sons of God. Go through this list and see if there is anything you might recognize in your own heart. I had to work on anger for quite a while but now it is not a problem. When you find something in your own heart, ask the Holy Spirit to take it away and replace it with the positive and usually opposite characteristic.

For instance the Holy Spirit placed in me bowels of mercy, a mercy gift, in place of the anger I had learned as a child growing up. Thank God for the wisdom and prayers of the Holy Spirit!

The enemy is always looking for opportunities to attack us. I remember experiencing so many attacks that I finally made some promises to myself and said:

"Well, if I have been born into a war zone, I'd better learn to fight. I refuse to do anything without consulting the Holy Spirit and the Word first and I WILL continue in prayer until I hear from God. Then I WILL obey what God says. I will learn to be a good soldier."

Our Spiritual Language Confuses the Enemy.

The devil has no right or access into our born-again spirit. Neither does the devil have any say in the process of edification and mortification that the Holy Spirit is performing in us. As soon as you recognize that the enemy is trying to get you off track, or neutralize your spiritual growth, take authority over those devils. You must kick him out of your life and mean business. He will not leave you alone if he thinks he can still convince you to quit praying or to sin. I thank my God that His ways are higher and Jesus has already won all our battles for us. We must know our God and take our stand against all attacks of the enemy.

As we continue praying in the spirit, those mysteries hidden in the word will begin to open up to us and there is great joy as we continue to receive the revelations in the word. As we press through our fleshly strongholds, we are growing step by step and the Holy Spirit lights the path ahead of us. Because we have allowed the Holy Spirit to become our personal tutor and guide to help us, we can now begin to know our Father. We become more aware of His great love and kindness as we move into our inheritance as a son and worship Him for all He has given us. Private worship now becomes an important key in knowing our Father intimately. As we please the Father, His favor upon us becomes evident to others and to us.

Impasses in Prayer

An impasse is a spiritual wall that seems to prevent us from going any further into God. When we pray in tongues, it causes ugly things to arise from our soul. The Holy Spirit is showing us what we have inside us: strongholds of the flesh. These *strongholds* can be habits that we had developed over time. A spiritual battle ensues between our soul and our spirit. We must press through these times. The Word of God in the Psalms can offer us consolation. If you will rejoice and worship God for who He is and what He has done, eventually you will come to a place of supernatural peace and that area of flesh will be mortified forever!

Usually our *first impasse* is getting past the enemy's attempts to take us out of prayer. Praying in the spirit will eventually become a daily habit. The Holy Spirit will work our spiritual maturity as we surrender our flesh nature to God. The Holy Spirit will encourage us to continue in the purging process in our soul. He has become my most trusted friend during this edification process as I mature in Christ. 2 Corinthians 6:17-7:1 gives us a clearer view:

Wherefore come out from among them, and be ye separate, saith the Lord, and touch not the unclean thing; and I will receive you, and will be a Father unto

you, and ye shall be my sons and daughters, saith the Lord Almighty. Having therefore these promises, dearly beloved, let us cleanse ourselves from all filthiness of the flesh and spirit, perfecting holiness in the fear of God.

Filthiness of Flesh, Soul and Spirit

There are three areas the Holy Spirit begins to clean up inside of us: filthiness of BODY, SOUL and SPIRIT. Generally, the first area the Holy Spirit begins to work on *is filthiness of body.* These are some examples of strongholds of the flesh or body: smoking, drinking and partying, pornography, perverse sexual habits and anything that can harm our physical body. These sins do harm to our body which is the temple of God. They can also harm the people that we love who care about us. These sins can also be the addictions that our flesh craves. I found out that if we don't kill these harmful desires, they CAN kill us.

When we take a stand against these sins, God begins to show us the root cause and the Holy Spirit will help lead us out of the stronghold or addiction. Jesus has mountains of grace available to anyone who agrees with God's word that *Sin shall not have dominion over me. (Romans 6:14)* Fasting will add power to mortify the works of the flesh. We can escape the pull of these fleshly addictions with God as our helper, just don't stop praying.

Next, the Holy Spirit begins to work in the area of *the soul*, which includes our mind, thoughts, will and emotions. Negative emotions empower negative thoughts creating strongholds in our soul. Lust comes as a thought that, when it is acted upon, becomes sin which brings forth death.

Emotions Need Not Rule Over Our Spirit.

Usually it is the emotions that cause many of us to fall into sin and keep us locked up in a perpetual cycle of defeat. Emotions cannot be dismissed; they need to be turned from toxic unhealthy emotions like anger to healthy expressions like worship. The Holy Spirit will bring us a song or laughter, even crying can help us. The emotional crutches we have used in the past such as blaming others, drinking, sex, drugs etc. are not healthy. God is trying to save us. If we continue to pray in tongues, the Holy Spirit will bring forward those unhealthy thoughts and emotions during our prayer time so that we can mortify it, then we can re-direct our emotions by worshipping God and receive healing for our soul. We can learn to worship God in the midst of our trials. Worship becomes warfare. Paul and Silas did that in prison. (Acts 16:25)

If we don't want to deal with something, usually we will tend to fall into self-justification saying to ourselves, "it's not so bad" or "I think its ok". When we find ourselves beginning to justify our actions we stop the purging process that the Holy Spirit is performing within our soul. Recognize that a stronghold is dying. Take responsibility and humble yourself. Repent, then you will be rid of that ugly thing forever. Pray and fast if you need to.

Recognize that whatever we are willing to justify, we are not willing to mortify. Our will needs to line up with God's will. We must get to the place where we hate sin as much as God does. Unfortunately, this is often the place where people will stop praying in tongues. Inside us a battle is raging! Our old nature, like a spoiled child, is saying, "It's mine, it's mine and I won't give it up." This should confirm beyond a doubt that we DO INDEED have a stronghold in our soul that must go. There is freedom and remember that *our new nature* IS stronger than our flesh. The Word and the spirit always win if you don't quit praying in tongues, confessing the Word & using the keys. (See pages 41-43)

Strongholds will come down. When we first come up against a stronghold we may feel like we are flying apart like a cheap watch, but if we continue to pray in tongues and press through those feelings. Then the Holy Spirit will come with His grace and remove that thing from our life forever. Sometimes we feel like we are going to die, but it is just a lying emotion! So don't give in to feelings. Keep praying in tongues. It will pass.

God Wants Pure Motives in Our Heart.

The Holy Spirit will also deal with our heart's motives and why we do what we do. *God never thinks evil, so those evil thoughts about others have to go.* God is love and we are becoming like our Father. Things like jealousy, envy, unforgiveness and other soul issues are being replaced as we are conformed to the image of God within us.

The soul encompasses mind, emotions and our will. Confession of the Word is another tool that can bring us truth where a lie used to be. When we personalize a scripture (promise from God) and believe it, we make it our own and receive power from God to confront Satan's lies with truth. I found out that I had believed many lies about myself. I took Romans 8:1 in my mouth and repeated it over and over, out loud, until I believed it:

There is, therefore, now no condemnation to those who are in Christ Jesus, who walk not after the flesh but after the spirit.

Torment from the enemy left me, faith rose up inside me and God came into my circumstances. But that emotional war in the **soul** can be tough, so train yourself to use the key of worship along with confession as you take possession of His promises for your life and be encouraged; God is greater than your own heart.(1 John 3:20-22)

For if our heart condemn us, God is greater than our heart, and knoweth all things. Beloved if our heart condemn us not, then have we confidence toward God, and whatsoever we ask, we receive of Him, because we keep His commandments, and do those things that are pleasing in His sight.

Be Watchful and Ready

Attacks at level three usually come in the form of wolves and temptations of the flesh. The devil will send to us what our flesh desires hoping we will choose the flesh again. If you fall, run to Jesus and just keep getting up again and again. Eventually, the devil will become convinced that you cannot be tempted in that area any more. Paul never got comfortable with his flesh.

Wolves are predators. They can enter into your life as "friends" even in the church. We must separate ourselves from those who come to take advantage of our fleshly weaknesses tempting us to draw back into sinful ways. We must stand against sin and treat our flesh violently doing things that will convince our soul and the devil that we mean business. Continue to worship God and pray in tongues. Confess the Word to yourself and to the devil. Use the keys! Keep at it until the devil goes away and God's presence and peace comes. 1 John 1:9-10 says:

If we confess our sins, He is faithful and just to forgive us our sins, and to cleanse us from all unrighteousness. If we say that we have not sinned we make him a liar and his Word is not in us.

There is a third area where we need purging by the Holy Spirit. This is the area of *filthiness of spirit* which is wrong beliefs. Religion and false doctrines have influenced us and almost all of us have believed some lies about God. Until we received our new spirit from Jesus, these lies about God and idolatry were tolerated by God. The Spirit of God is the Spirit of Truth in us so that we can no longer continue to live believing lies about God.

I was brought up Roman Catholic. When I got saved, I had some questions about the doctrines I had learned there. You might have had other experiences. The Holy Spirit began to reveal to me those things that did not agree with His Word. The Lord will expose any false doctrine in the light of the Word. I am so grateful to God for leading and guiding me into truth. Wrong believing can be deadly. Cults have killed people in the name of religion.

Men will teach what they have been taught by other men but it may not be truth from the Word of God. We can know the truth when we learn to meditate and assimilate the Word of God, always keeping verses within its context. Hebrews 4:12 speaks about the ability of the Word of God to correct us in doctrine and truth.

For the Word of God is quick and powerful, and sharper than any two edged sword, piercing even to the

dividing asunder of soul and spirit, and of the joints and marrow, and is a discerner of the thoughts and intents of the heart.

Read the bible daily. Smith Wigglesworth never let an hour pass without reading something from the Word. Being filled with truth will keep away the lies. Satan is a very good liar. If there is any question, the Word will discern it for you. Go to the Word.

Mortification of Old Nature Brings Power

We come through this level of purging with great benefits and the ugly stuff is gone and burned up forever. This is really good news for those who had problems with addiction and strongholds of the flesh. If we give our junk to God He will remove it from us and we will be changed forever. Now we can rejoice because we are really changing. He wants to purge out the desire for sin in us with his holy fire. In Matthew 3:11-13 John speaks of that fire.

I indeed baptize you with water unto repentance: but he that cometh after me is mightier than I, whose shoes I am not worthy to bear: He shall baptize you with the Holy Ghost and with fire; whose fan is in His hand and He will thoroughly purge his floor and gather His wheat into the garner; but He will burn up the chaff with unquenchable fire.

Jesus and the Holy Spirit came to destroy our old nature of sin in the flesh and gather out the fruit of righteousness to the Father. This is their work of sanctification.

Level Four - Disciples

As we become disciples (disciplined followers of Christ), we begin to look more like sons of God and less like sheep. The transformation of our mind is taking place as we put on the mind of Christ. 1 Corinthians 2:16 explains:

For who hath known the mind of the Lord, that he may instruct him? But we have the mind of Christ.

Included in our new nature we received from Christ is the mind of Christ. We can learn how to access the mind of Christ within us and submit ourselves in love to God's will for us. 1 Corinthians 1:9-10:

God is faithful, by whom ye were called unto the fellowship of his Son Jesus Christ our Lord. Now I beseech you, brethren, by the name of our Lord Jesus Christ, that ye all speak the same thing and that there be no divisions among you; but that ye be perfectly joined together in the same mind and in the same judgment.

Love binds us together as a corporate body. Other people become more important to us as we come together in unity. We go through battles together and we suffer together. So did the early church. The first Christians were recognized by the love of God in them. Likewise we submit ourselves one to another in the love of God and respect one another. As we die to self, we become more of a family. We have much to learn about the Kingdom of God.

Attacks of the enemy at level four are dealing mostly with our heart motives. Jesus knew that the condition of our heart would determine what we will or won't do. There must be a fundamental change of heart as we mature.

Jesus teaches us that our heart condition and heart motives are what allow that seed of truth to grow and bear fruit. In the parable of the seed and the sower Jesus explains our growth. He begins by telling us that this is the foundation and understanding of all parables. It shows us how we are to grow up and the things we must get past to become sons of God.

The Foundation of all Parables is The Condition of Our Heart

In Mark chapter 4, verses 13-20, Jesus describes four types of ground. The ground is our heart condition. The seed is the Word we receive.

And He said unto them, know ye not this parable? And how then will ye know all parables? The sower soweth the word. And these are they
1) By the wayside, where the word is sown; but when they have heard, Satan cometh immediately, and taketh away the word that was sown in their hearts. And these are they likewise which are sown on
2) stony ground; who when they have heard the word, immediately receive it with gladness; and have no root in themselves, and so endure but for a time; and afterward, when affliction or persecution arises for the word's sake, immediately they are offended. And these are they which are

3) sown among thorns; such as hear the word and the cares of this world and the deceitfulness of riches and the lusts of other things entering in, choke the word, and it becomes unfruitful. And these are they which

4) receive it, and bring forth fruit, some thirtyfold, some sixty and some an hundred.

All of us have to get past the things mentioned in this parable and clean our hearts from the influences Jesus is speaking about. In Jesus' first example: by the wayside, he says that Satan comes immediately to steal the Word from our heart. We must be on guard to protect and keep the Word so that if God spoke something to us whether in prophecy or in a teaching, we will write it down, take it to God and wait on God, meditating on that Word. If it is direction, we can put it in the form of a confession and make it our own until it comes to pass in our life. I refuse to let the devil steal what God has given to me. Stewardship of the Word is just as important as stewardship of money and things, if not far more important.

In the second example there was no root and the seed was sown but when it grew up there was little depth of growth. The rocky soil (offenses) prevented that person from putting down deep roots. Time spent with God in prayer will grow a tap root that reaches deep into the living water of the river of life. Some people have a shallow root system that washes away in a storm. In this parable, Jesus says that offences will come so we must learn to forgive others from the heart and also ourselves. When we begin to know the power and depth of the love of God, we can forgive. Our father wants us unshakable in the storms.

In Jesus' third example, thorns come up and choke the word. He shows us three things: Cares of this world, deceitfulness of riches and lust for other things.

1. Cares of this world include people who worry about everything. Some people are caught up in the worries of life. Jesus tells us not to worry but instead we can learn to trust in God for our provision. He honors faith and trust in Him, not fear and worry. It is a time waster and a trap. We must learn how to cast our cares over onto Jesus. Again, pray and give it over to God continually.

2. Deceitfulness of riches. I found that money has a power over the human soul that can be very deceitful. God calls the love of money the root of all evil. The Bible says that it is impossible to serve both God and mammon. In our heart we will treasure the one or the other. God is always concerned about our heart. Choose Jesus over money.

3. Lust for other things. These lusts must be mortified. Here in America, it is a major trap of the enemy to buy more than we can afford, feeding our old carnal nature. We must learn to be content with what we have and not allow the enemy to tempt us in this way.

Just like thorns, these daily life concerns choke our spiritual life and our fruitfulness for God's kingdom. It is ok to struggle and learn. There is grace for that, but now we must get past these obstacles to spiritual maturity. The Holy Spirit is willing to pray for us if we will give Him what He needs, our time in prayer. It will pay off if you put God first. It's never too late to get back on track and grow.

Level Five - Sons of God Dressed for Battle

God wants our perfection, our maturity. We know that we are weak but God is strong. Paul said that He was glad when he was weak and others were strong. He knew the substitution principal of grace; that it is God's grace that comes to us in those times of need. The more we die to our own strength (our flesh nature) the more power we receive from God. We are also charged to press forward, forgetting the past as this holy exchange takes place in us.

In the illustration on page 44, I have depicted the sons of God dressed in the armor of God with the anointing and glory that accompanies it. When I first heard that someone else had seen the anointing on me, I was shocked. I wondered what they saw. I didn't feel any different nor did I see great miracles, but something had happened to me as a result of obeying God and praying in tongues. I had a new boldness to confront the devil and his works. Ephesians 6:10-13 gives us an image of God's armor:

Finally, my brethren, be strong in the Lord and in the power of His might. Put on the whole armor of God that ye may be able to stand against the wiles of the devil. For we wrestle not against flesh and blood, but against principalities, against powers, against the rulers of the darkness of this world, against spiritual wickedness in high places. Wherefore take unto you the whole armor of God that ye may be able to withstand in the evil day, and having done all, to stand.

Paul uses the example of armor to teach us to walk in truth, righteousness, peace and faith. We understand that we have an enemy lurking nearby to devour us if we should get lazy or complacent. The enemy assaults our minds with thoughts to talk us into quitting the pursuit of God and maturity. The sword (Word of God) is an aggressive weapon used to cut off and separate soul from spirit and to fight the devil as Jesus did in the desert with truth from the Word of God.

When we fight, it is necessary to understand how to fight and what the war is. The war is against our own flesh and the devil. We cannot fight the devil on his terms, nor can we come up against him face to face. The next verse (Ephesians 6:18) tells us how to fight. We are to pray in the spirit and intercede for our brothers and sisters.

...Praying always with all prayer and supplication in the spirit (tongues), and watching thereunto with all perseverance and supplication for all saints.

We do not war after the flesh. Our wrestling is on the inside not on the outside. We have a new nature so now the only way the devil can tempt us to sin is when we disobey God and get in the flesh. Our fight is the fight of faith, believing God's work and dominion over sin and death. We are to walk in the new and living way, after the power of an endless life from Jesus. Jesus never battled with principalities; He used his authority to cast out devils. They knew him and feared Him. Devils still do fear Jesus in us. Jesus never subjected Himself to flesh, demons or man but He learned obedience and walked in the authority He was given by the Father. Jesus preached the Kingdom. Paul explained this warfare more clearly in 2 Corinthians 10:2-7:

> ...some which think of us as if we walked according to the flesh, for though we walk in the flesh, we do not war after the flesh: for the weapons of our warfare are not carnal, but mighty through God to the pulling down of strongholds; casting down imaginations, and every high thing that exalteth itself against the knowledge of God, and bringing into captivity every thought to the obedience of Christ; and having in readiness to revenge all disobedience, when your obedience is fulfilled. Do you look on things after the outward appearance?

Imaginations, thoughts and temptations come to us through our carnal mind. Deception comes through the mind also. Much of the doctrinal error regarding spiritual warfare comes from an Old Testament instead of New Testament mentality and foundation of the Word. We are born again and we should be living *in resurrection life* with Jesus. There remains a kind of veil over our understanding when we spend more time in the Old Testament than in the words and sayings of Jesus, which, after His crucifixion is now *our covenant*. In Christ we are new creatures. Many of the parables of Jesus were warnings to the Jews about not discerning the time of the coming of Jesus, the Messiah and the new covenant.

Jesus' coming changed the world entirely. His nature in us has made us sons. His victory over sin made many things available to us. Old Testament saints did not have a new nature from God; they had only the law and a promise of the Messiah to come. Understanding and believing these foundational truths will change the way you look at things, your position in Christ and how you grow in your new nature. That is why we meditate and assimilate *only* the New Testament first until *that* foundation is firmly established inside our spirit. Our authority comes from Jesus, not Moses.

Our enemy will come at level five as an angel of light to deceive us. He will attempt to bring us into bondage under false apostles, false prophets or get us to believe false doctrine. The doctrine of Gnosticism almost neutralized the entire early church. If we are not careful, we too can be deceived. One degree off the straight and narrow path now can lead us far away from the truth later. *We must be careful to stay teachable and open to correction.* Many of today's denominations have accepted some form of doctrinal error.

Christ in You: The Hope of Glory

One of the greatest mysteries revealed to me is in Colossians 1:26-27, the mystery of the new nature being manifested in us, which is, *"Christ in you, the hope of glory."*

Even the mystery which hath been hid from ages and from generations, but now is made manifest to His saints: to whom God would make known what is the riches of the glory of this mystery among the gentiles; which is Christ in you; the hope of glory.

The mystery of the DNA of God in me gives me hope. I had no idea what God had placed in me when I got saved. Because of Christ's nature in me, I can be identified by the Spirit at my time of resurrection. I have God's seal in my bones. I can receive a glorified body. I am chosen to receive supernatural gifts from God. I can hear God. Christ in us makes it possible for us to be sons of God. His love in me changes me so that now I can see more of His plan unfolding as I approach maturity. My inheritance is a great hope to hold on to. In John 15:13-17 Jesus says:

Greater love hath no man than this that a man lay down his life for his friends, you are my friends, if ye do whatsoever I command you. Henceforth I call you not servants; for the servant knows not what his lord doeth; but I have called you friends; for all things that I have heard of my Father I have made known unto you. Ye have not chosen me, but I have chosen you and ordained you, that you should go and bring forth fruit and that your fruit should remain; that whatsoever ye shall ask of the Father in my name, He may give it you. These things I command you, that you love one another.

Jesus' commandment is to love one another. At this higher level of spiritual growth, we are beginning to come to a place in our walk with God where we can be trusted by God not to hurt each other and we will obey Him when He speaks. We have fought the good fight of faith and believed his Word.

Gifts of Spirit Qualify Our Calling

The gifts of the spirit in Ephesians 4:8 (below) are given to do the work of the Lord and we are sent out to heal the sick, raise the dead and cast out devils, in Jesus name. We discover what our calling (vocation) is and we set out to fulfill His will in our life. 1 Corinthians 12:8-10 says:

Wherefore He saith, when He ascended up on high, He led captivity captive, and gave gifts unto men.

Briefly, the nine gifts of the spirit can be divided into three categories, each having a separate and distinct purpose.

1.) *The five-fold ministries* (apostles, prophets, evangelist, pastor, and teacher) are set aside for the purpose of perfecting the saints and the gifts that empower them are needed to carry out this purpose.

2.) The operations of the ministry of *helps and governments* have been given those gifts necessary to achieve that particular work. These gifts enable any church or minister to carry out the call God has placed on their heart. There are bills to be paid and things to be administered to get the Word out and souls saved. God sets these people in the church to do that work and to empower them with gifts such as supernatural wisdom.

3.) The eighth operation includes the four *diversities of tongues,* each having a separate set of rules that govern their use. For instance, tongues to be interpreted as prophecy has different rules than tongues for personal edification or tongues for intercession, or as a sign to the unbeliever. Prophecy is given to build up the church.

Tongues for personal edification are given to everyone to build up the personal spiritual life of the believer. The four diversities are explained in 1 Corinthians 14 and Romans 8:26. A detailed explanation of the operation of these diversities can be found in Dave Roberson's Book, <u>The Walk of the Spirit, The Walk of Power</u>.

At level five, the enemy will use wrong teachings and false doctrines to confuse us and get us off track or discourage us, if possible. You will know those who are true apostles and prophets by their fruit and the gifts in operation. There is an anointing (power) on their lives.

The fruit of the spirit is love, joy, peace, longsuffering, gentleness, goodness, faith, meekness and temperance. True apostles and prophets are known by these fruits; they are chosen by God and empowered with the necessary gifts to complete their call. They are tested as Paul was. These true servants will feed your spirit, not your flesh. They will do us good, not harm. We can trust Christ to provide for us a good spiritual covering. We do not need to fear. But we know that men are not perfect so the scripture tells us that prophecy is subject to the prophet. All of us are in training but know that God tests the heart. The test of a prophet is that the prophecies he speaks come from God and they always come to pass.

False apostles and prophets usually proclaim their own position in the church. A true prophet or apostle does not need to announce his office by putting a title before his name, rather he is known by the fruit of his life before God and men. Titles are not from God, they are from men. We should test the spirits. (1 John 4:1) Spectacular things are not always from God. False apostles will attempt to control the church. They can bring in false doctrine. The Holy Spirit inside our spirit can discern the truth.

Warnings from the Early Church

Paul tells us in Jude 4 and in verses 18-20 what to look for in the character of these deceivers that sought to ruin the faith of the early church:

For there are certain men who crept into the church unawares, ungodly men turning the grace of our

God into lasciviousness and denying the only Lord God, and our Lord Jesus Christ.

... there should be mockers in the last time, who should walk after their own ungodly lusts. These be they who separate themselves, sensual, having not the spirit. But ye beloved, building up yourselves on your most holy faith, praying in the Holy Ghost, looking for the mercy of our Lord Jesus Christ unto eternal life.

The scripture not only tells us what the problem is but also exactly how to win against these evil attacks of the enemy by building ourselves up over it all, praying in the spirit; in tongues. These men were sensual and not led by the spirit. They denied the Lord and turned the grace of God into filthiness. Today some people call that sloppy grace. Sloppy grace is when people use grace as an excuse to continue in their sin instead of allowing the power of God to get them out of their sin. If anyone really wants to quit sinning God will help them, but He cannot bless sin.

The gift of tongues is given to help us mature. Yet there are still people who do not have this gift or the power of God operating for them. Hear what the Lord is saying and enter into the fullness of God and receive from Jesus in His own words in First John 2:18 and John 16:33:

Little children, it is the last time: and as ye have heard that antichrist shall come, even now are there many antichrists; whereby we know that it is the last time.
These things I have spoken unto you, that in me ye might have peace. In the world ye shall have tribulation: but be of good cheer: I have overcome the world.

Level Six - Agape love

Agape love is God's unconditional love and it is our goal and final step into maturity and glory. There is a greater glory for the sons of God than there was for Moses under the Old Testament. I don't know where your spiritual walk is but I do know that your Father loves you greatly. He would not have gone to all that trouble to reach you unless He planned for you to go all the way into full maturity as a son of God. God has an inheritance and reward for you.

Love is the final goal. God's very character is love. Agape love is that kind of love that is unselfish, more than friendship, not the sensual kind of human love but a self-sacrificing love. God naturally wants all his children to be like him and to mature in this kind of love. Agape love is not something that comes naturally to us but we can learn to be like him. The Love chapter (paraphrased) of First Corinthians 13:4-8 reveals God's character of love.

Charity (love) suffers long and is kind. Love does not envy and does not vaunt itself. It is not easily puffed up in pride. Love never behaves itself unseemly, seeks not her own and is not easily provoked. Love thinks no evil and does not rejoice when someone sins or fails but rejoices in the truth. Love bears all things, believes all things, hopes all things and endures all things. Love never fails.

The Word says that perfect love casts out fear. When we are able to walk in the love of God, there will be no fear.

At level six we are come to a place in our spiritual growth where the flesh nature in us is not as much of an issue as it was when we first began. I call this getting past the *veil of the flesh*. We cannot come into agape love until our "self" (old selfish nature) is rendered dead. We have placed our body as a living sacrifice on God's altar (Romans 12:1) and asked him to kill anything inside us that would impede our development as a son of God. At this level we qualify to be chosen, not just called of God. Jesus taught his disciple this kind of love. In 1 Peter 4:1-2 Peter writes:

Forasmuch then as Christ hath suffered for us in the flesh, arm yourselves likewise with the same mind; for he that hath suffered in the flesh hath ceased from sin that he should no longer live the rest of his time in the flesh to the lusts of men, but to the will of God.

The only thing the devil can do at this point is act out his rage for his time is short. By now we know most of his tricks and we know that he uses our flesh nature if he can. So we can wait for our Lord's coming with joy and confidence that Our God who began a good work in us will bring it to completion. Matthew 24:23-25 warns us:

Then if any shall say unto you, Lo, here is Christ, or there; believe it not. For there shall arise false prophets, and shall show great signs and wonders; insomuch that, if it were possible, they shall deceive the very elect. Behold I have told you before.

Antichrists and false prophets, false signs and wonders are also signs of the time before Jesus returns. Knowing what is up ahead, we can prepare ourselves for these things and be watchful. It will not be possible to deceive us in the last days before Jesus returns if we are led by the spirit.

There is a glory that Jesus received for obeying the Father. There is also a glory waiting for us who will obey Jesus. Do you remember that Adam was clothed with glory in the garden? The Holy Spirit was sent to administer glory to us and through us. He comes to us as a seal and deposit of God's power when we receive the baptism in the Holy Ghost. He has come to help us become sons of God. It is not automatic; we must choose to receive the power of God and the gifts of the spirit, knowing that God gives good gifts to those He loves.

Moses was given a glory while experiencing the presence of God on Mount Sinai. That was the glory of the law, but now you and I have been chosen to receive a greater glory; to partake of God's very nature. Moses' glory is called the ministry of death and our glory is called the ministry of righteousness administered by the Holy Spirit Himself, as it says in 2 Corinthians 3:7-11.

But if the ministration of death, written and engraven in stones was glorious, so that the children of Israel could not stedfastly behold the face of Moses for the glory of his countenance; which glory was to be done away; How shall not the ministration of the spirit be rather glorious? For if the ministration of condemnation be glory, much more doth the ministration of righteousness exceed in glory, for even that which was made glorious had no glory in this respect, by reason of the glory that excelleth. For if that which is done away was glorious, much more that which remaineth is glorious.

Can you see that there is more on the horizon for us who will follow Jesus and recognize the times we live in? It is easier to remain a child but it is not beneficial. We must lay aside childish things and our own desires so that we can help others to know our Lord and Father. Parents will sacrifice for their children. Jesus gave his life for us out of love for us, now we can sacrifice for our brothers and sisters to know God.

We Overcome By Our Testimony and Word

In this last level of growth, praying in tongues and a lifestyle of prayer has become part of us like it was with Jesus. We are forever connected to the Father and the Spirit. We are one. The keys that I presented here have become a meeting place of delight and fellowship with our Lord. We are becoming one together in the love of God. We are also becoming one as they are one; Father, Son and Holy Spirit. Here is Jesus' prayer for us in John 17:21.

That they all may be one, as thou Father, art in me, and I in thee, that they also may be one in Us: that the world may believe that Thou hast sent me.

Paul reminds us in Galatians 2:20 of our position in Christ by faith.

I am crucified with Christ: nevertheless I live; yet not I, but Christ liveth in me: and the life I now live in the flesh I live by the faith of the Son of God, who loved me and gave Himself for me.

We overcome all things by Jesus' blood and by our own testimony. In the end, it is what we do with what we have been given that decides what we will be. The angels in heaven boast of our great victory in Revelation 12:10-11:

And I heard a loud voice saying in heaven, Now is come salvation, and strength, and the kingdom of our God, and the power of his Christ: for the accuser of our brethren is cast down, which accused them before our God day and night. And they overcame him by the blood of the Lamb and by the word of their testimony; and they loved not their lives unto death.

Conclusion

We should never try to do anything apart from Jesus, If we get out of His will, we quickly recognize that it was His grace and favor that got us this far and we can do nothing without Him. Growing up without the Holy Spirit is the same as growing up without Jesus. Both are God and indispensable. 1 Corinthians 13:11.

When I was a child, I spake as a child, I understood as a child, I thought as a child: but when I became a man, I put away childish things.

The gifts of the Spirit are vital to maturity. Without the Holy Spirit we cannot become sons of God. Jesus walked in the power of God and supernatural abilities but His flesh nature was weak like ours. He was completely dependent on the Holy Spirit while He was living here on earth. This intimate cooperation with the Holy Spirit is key to our maturity. We cannot know the things of God except by the leadership of the Holy Spirit and *His prayers though us* maturing our new nature and mortifying our old nature.

Old Testament Living Cannot Bring Us into New Testament Maturity as Sons

There were no born again people before Christ came, so all Old Testament believers did not have Christ's nature in them. They came to God under the Old Covenant. But we are born again and there is only one way for us to become mature sons of God: *by the Spirit.* There are no longer two covenants, there is only one. The covenant made with Jesus Christ by which we are to live and to which we must conform: the covenant of the born again man. Hebrews 10:9 & 10 clearly explain that the first covenant has been replaced by the New Covenant in Jesus' blood.

The said he, Lo, I come to do thy will, O God. He taketh away the first that he may establish the second. By the which will we are sanctified through the offering of the body of Jesus Christ once for all.

The Pharisees could not discern the time of Christ. They looked for supernatural signs seeking to affirm their social position. This was a grave error, for *eternal life* comes only by Jesus Christ.

There are two groups of people that persecute true believers:
1.) Those who continue to live under the Old Testament law instead of the grace that came by Jesus Christ and,
2.) Those that hate Christ and are led by a spirit of anti-Christ. They deny that Jesus has come in the flesh.

Those under the law use the law to control others for their own selfish motives. Jesus' enemies were the religious leaders of the day. They would use the law to deny Jesus as Messiah. *"How can you heal on the Sabbath? It is against the law,"* they would say. They did not understand the meaning behind the law. They substituted legalism for righteousness.

We need to understand that the purpose of the Old Testament law was to reveal to man that he had a sinful NATURE and COULD NOT keep the laws of God.

Antichrist spirits operating through men also bring persecution to Christ's followers. These people bring false teachings of men and they hate Christians because they do not have a new nature. These are religions not based on the truth of who God is: Communism, Islam and others. But good exposes evil. We know where these teachings come from because we know the devil comes to kill, steal and destroy. Jesus said Satan was *a murderer* from the beginning. These people have the nature of the Evil One and they do not believe that Jesus is who He says He is.

We Must Choose to Cooperate with God's Work

Under the guidance of the Holy Spirit, we choose to surrender our spirit for maturity, put off our old nature of lust and pride and walk under the leadership of the Holy Spirit. The time has come to hear and see Jesus with our new nature. We choose to obey the Holy Spirit when He speaks to us. We choose to speak in tongues to hear God. We surrender ourselves for training and maturing into sonship toward holiness.

To deny the gift of God is to disobey God because He has no other plan for our maturity. The Holy Spirit was the power behind the miracles of Jesus. He is the power we need to mature also. What can God do if His hands are tied? How can He speak to us? God is a spirit. He sent the Holy Spirit to teach us, lead us and guide us in God's ways. We cannot know God by the written word alone. We need to experience God for ourselves. We have been sent the third person of the Godhead from Jesus and the Father to perfect us in our new nature.

The ministry of the Holy Spirit is to lead and guide us into all truth because we are "blinded" by the flesh.

Jesus spoke of our weaknesses in the parable of the seed and sower. He shows us the things we must overcome in our heart. These are the obstacles we must get past. The devil will come and tempt us to draw back into the strongholds and operations of the flesh.

Legalism under Old Testament law can hold us back from maturity and keep us in condemnation and bondage as much as fleshly lusts and desires. We willingly submit these things to God and mortify those fleshly desires knowing it will result in a life of freedom.

The ministry of the Holy Spirit as the Comforter brings us consolation and healing in our times of need and His joy in times of sorrow. He brings healing to us in our emotions and in our soul. The supernatural gifts of laughter and intercession help us through times of stress and persecution.

There are many "gifts of the Spirit" given to help us in our walk with God into sonship. We receive from God our Father *by inheritance* through Christ by grace. It is given to us. It cannot be earned. Jesus has provided for us our salvation from sin and death, prosperity of soul, the gifts of the Spirit, and the earnest deposit of the Holy Spirit to empower us for ministry, holiness and maturity. God has high expectations for us according to Hebrews 12:22-24:

But ye are come unto mount Zion, and unto the city of the living God, the heavenly Jerusalem, and to the innumerable company of angels, to the general assembly and church of the firstborn, which are written in heaven, and to God the Judge of all, and to the spirits of just men made perfect, and to Jesus the mediator of the new covenant, and to the blood of sprinkling, that speaks better things than Abel.

Herein is the Problem

We have the mind of Christ but we don't know how to use it. We have the nature of Christ but it has not been developed. We need to learn how to operate as sons of God as Jesus did without sin and in power. Without the ministry and work of the Holy Spirit operating in us, this is impossible, but *with God* all things are possible.

I am just now beginning to see how much unbelief and how little truth we as believers are operating in. As we worship Him in spirit and truth we draw near to know God as He really is. That truth will set us so free. But if we stay in bondage to Old Testament legalistic thinking and the flesh nature then we will never know the freedom of sonship and the joy of inheritance.

Jacob went through a lot to get his inheritance. It caused him to die to self and gain the name Israel. The believers in the book of Acts also paid a high price to know God the Father and do His will.

Now each of us must decide how much we will value this inheritance. Do we consider our Lord's sacrifice a very valuable thing? Do we value our inheritance of eternal life and our sonship? Yes, I think we agree it is most valuable! And you are very valuable to the Father also. You are His inheritance.

A Parable of Ten Virgins

In Matthew 24, Jesus gives us signs of the end of our age. Then In Matthew 25, He gives us three parables: the parable of the ten virgins, the parable of the talents given to his servants, and separation of sheep and goats.

Of the ten virgins, five were wise and prepared for his coming but five were not prepared and were very late getting oil in their lamps. You could say they were very late in getting the anointing of the Holy Spirit in their lives. The master shut the door and said He did not know them.

Then Jesus gives us the parable of a man traveling to a far country that entrusted his goods to his servants and gave them five, two and one talent. Those who did something with those gifts were called good and faithful servants but those did nothing or little were called unprofitable.

Lastly, Jesus tells us that when He returns to judge the nations, He will separate the sheep from the goats. Here He marks a distinct difference in the nature of the obedient sheep and the bucking goat. The sheep have compassion and love working through them but the goats were not operating in mercy and compassion. It will be evident which one we are by our fruits.

We must have a new nature and it must be developed to be useful. The old man has been declared dead and the new man will be perfected in his nature. The goats looked out for themselves but sheep have learned to operate in the love of God. They will pray for their enemies and do Jesus' sayings. In these parables I find three things:

1. A warning that He is returning for those He knows.

2. A warning that we must continue to be ready and watchful in prayer with the Holy Spirit anointing.

3. When He does return He will reward those who have sought Him out diligently.

For the Son of Man shall come in the glory of his Father with his angels; and then he shall reward every man according to his works.

Matthew 16:27 tells us that there is more than just being saved; there is also reward for those who diligently seek him. That reward could affect our position in eternity. I would hate to be told that He doesn't even know me. I do want to be told I have been a good and faithful servant and I would like to be known for the mercy and compassion I have shown to the hurting ones.

This book has only presented some of the basic principles of maturity in Christ. Please notice that God's end goal is the sanctification (perfection) of the sons of God operating in the love of God, not religion. This is accomplished as we obey God and receive all He has given us. As we learn to use the keys on pages 41-43, we can grow in our spirit and overcome our weaknesses. May God bless you and help you in all that you are called to do for our Lord Jesus Christ and may your reward be great and your life richly blessed.

Appendix A

Prayer of Salvation

Before we can be filled with the Holy Spirit and receive his supernatural gift of tongues, our human spirit must be born again in Jesus Christ. The new nature you will receive frees you from the curse of sin and imparts to you the free gift of eternal life with God. The Holy Spirit, who is your Helper, can then come to give you evidence of heaven's power as a son of God.

Do you believe that Jesus died for your sins and rose again to give you eternal life? Would you like to receive Him as Lord and Savior right now? If so, please pray the following prayer from your heart:

Dear Lord Jesus, Please come into my heart and forgive me of my sins. I want to be born again. I receive you now as my personal Lord and Savior. I know I have made wrong decisions and sinned against you. Please take over my life. Cleanse me from all my unrighteousness and give me your righteousness so I can trust in you and not in myself. I receive your free gift of eternal life and salvation. I receive your love for me. Thank you for saving me today. Amen.

Welcome to the family of God! Write down this day in your Bible. Read the Word of God as your daily food. You have received a new nature which is born from above. You are not of this world. You have a new family and inheritance. Continue to choose life over death, take the journey into full maturity and allow the Holy Spirit to be your Teacher and Helper. Get to know Him and trust in God to meet all your needs. Look for a good Bible believing church that will help you grow and live a victorious life as a child of God.

Now that you are clean and have a new nature you can receive the Holy Spirit as your Teacher. His job is to lead and guide you into all truth. You can pray the prayer in Appendix B and receive your inheritance. You don't have to wait. Jesus is the Living water your soul has been thirsting for. He wants you to overcome every obstacle but you need the help of the Holy Spirit.

Appendix B

Prayer to Receive the Baptism of the Holy Ghost

If you have never been baptized in the Holy Spirit or do not flow in your spiritual language, you can receive the baptism of the Holy Spirit. All you have to do is ask in faith for the Lord to fill you with the Holy Spirit and give you the gift of speaking in tongues.

The Holy Spirit will come upon you, and you will sense His presence. He will begin to fill your new nature with His spirit and create a new language on the inside of your spirit. When He does, your tongue and mouth will begin to shape the same words He is creating inside your spirit.

In John 1:23 John the Baptist says that Jesus is the baptizer of the Holy Spirit. Fix your inner vision on Him and pray this prayer:

Lord Jesus, baptize me in your Holy Spirit. I want to know my heavenly Father and receive power from on high. Thank you for giving me my new spiritual language to edify, to testify of Jesus and to build up my born again spirit. Thank you for gift of the Holy Spirit in my life. I receive this baptism of spirit, fill me now.

Now open your mouth and let the sounds come forth. Don't speak to God in your native language any longer. Yield yourself over to the presence of the Holy

Spirit, and begin to cry out to God in the words or sounds that come into your mouth.

It may sound like baby talk at first but when you continue to flow in it, the spirit will take over and you just continue to yield yourself to speaking the words the Holy Spirit gives you, you will begin to pull more of a flow out of your spirit. Soon you will be speaking fluently in your new supernatural language. Continue to pray in your new language for at least fifteen minutes to establish yourself in this gift you have just received.

Congratulations, you have just entered into a walk of power with God, the doorway into the supernatural realm of God!

If you still have questions see, *Hindrances to receiving the baptism in the Holy Spirit, Appendix 1* in the book, **_The Walk of the Spirit, The Walk of Power_** by Dave Roberson. This book and teachings are available in Spanish and other languages also and are free online at *www.daveroberson.org*.

Made in the USA
Charleston, SC
26 August 2013